Praying the Scriptures

Judson Cornwall

D1579401

Harvestime

Published in the United Kingdom by:
Harvestime Publishing Ltd, 69 Main Street,
Markfield, Leicester LE6 0UT

Scripture quotations are generally taken from the
New International Version. Copyright © 1978 by the
New York International Bible Society and published by
Hodder & Stoughton. Used by permission.

Other versions referred to:
Revised Authorised Version (RAV)

British Library Cataloguing in Publication Data

Cornwall, Judson
Praying the scriptures.
I. Title
248.32

ISBN 1-872877-05-2

Typeset and printed in the United Kingdom by:
Nuprint Ltd, Station Rd, Harpenden AL5 4SE

Contents

Dedication

To my six great-grandchildren, who are not only my heirs but heirs of God and joint-heirs with Jesus Christ.

Acknowledgements

This book was conceived in the heart of Bert Ghezzi, former editorial director of Creation House. It was enlarged by many members of the body of Christ, encouraged by my wife, Eleanor, laboriously thrust through the computer by my secretary, Terri Gargis, and, we feel, sweetly anointed by the Holy Spirit. How precious it is to be 'God's fellow-workers' (1 Corinthians 3:9).

Preface

Christianity is nothing without the Bible. Although there are many divisions among evangelicals, a common factor that unites Christians is belief in the God-breathed inspiration of the Scriptures. There is a firm commitment of faith that 'men spoke from God as they were carried along by the Holy Spirit' (2 Peter 1:21).

It would seem, however, that, although we hold the Scriptures to be sacred, we have almost prostituted them in the way we use them. The Bible is often turned to as a source of favourite quotations. It is used as the authority for pop-psychology or to undergird a personal philosophy of life. It is dissected, divided and dispensationalised to fit our way of thinking. Sometimes I wonder if God would even recognise his book – the way it is presented in some of our churches.

Even the ultra-fundamentalists seem to have missed the real design of the Bible. To them it is the source of material for sermons, but, as valuable as preaching is, God's book was given for a higher purpose than mere teaching.

The Bible is a *prayer book*. It commands us to pray – over two hundred and fifty times – and speaks of 'prayer,' 'prayers' and 'praying' an additional two hundred and eighty times. No doctrine that we preach is mentioned as many times as is prayer. Furthermore, the Bible gives repeated examples of great men and women praying, and many of those prayers are reported in the Scriptures.

Perhaps we have forgotten that Adam had no Bible; he had direct communication and communion with God. Through wilful disobedience, he forfeited this personal relationship and was driven from the garden and God's presence. This breach of fellowship so grieved God that he immediately began to offer a means of access to his presence to anyone who desired to commune with him.

The Bible is a record of God's restoring to humanity what was lost in Eden. The work of Christ at Calvary was far more than provision for the forgiveness of sins. The purpose of the cross has ever been to restore men and women to personal communication and fellowship with God.

God's Word to the holy men of Old Testament times was intended to reveal God and to offer a route of access to the heavenly Father. Of Jesus' birth it was declared, 'The Word became flesh and made his dwelling among us. We have seen his glory, the glory of the One and Only [margin – the Only Begotten], who came from the Father, full of grace and truth' (John 1:14). The written Word became the living Word, but the purpose of the Word remained the same – access to God. Christ is the Word incarnate; the Bible is the Word codified.

None would deny that the Bible is full of preaching material, but that isn't its prime purpose. The Word was given, both in written and living form, to return us to a personal relationship with Almighty God. Such a relationship, of course, demands communication, and prayer is communication with God.

The Bible, then, is a textbook on prayer. It teaches us the need to pray, the nature of prayer and the rewards of prayer. This is well-known. What seems to have been forgotten by some of today's generation is that the Bible can also become the very prayer we need to pray.

When we let the Bible become our prayer, we are praying an inspired vocabulary. It will often release deep inner feelings far better than extemporised prayers that come from our minds. God's Word is 'living and active. Sharper than any double-edged sword, it penetrates even to dividing soul and spirit, joints and marrow; it judges the thoughts and attitudes of the heart' (Hebrews 4:12). That which can discern and divide can certainly describe. Therefore, when used as the vehicle of our prayers, the Word of God is capable of declaring deep inner desires and thoughts of the soul-spirit.

It is my earnest desire that this book will stir the body of Christ to pray once again to God with the very words of God. It will breathe new life and authority into our praying.

Judson Cornwall
Phoenix, Arizona, USA
1990

1

Praying the Scriptures introduces us to prayer

Prayer is as natural to an individual as crying is to a baby. It is a reflex action of the human spirit. It almost requires a conscious action of the will to override this impulse. Children don't need to be taught to pray; they have to be taught *not* to pray, for they are comfortably accustomed to asking another to supply all their needs, and God is the greater 'another'.

But with the sophistication that comes with self-reliance, adults tend to negate the need for prayer, even though the desire remains latent within. A sunset, a storm brooding over the sea or the view from the rim of the Grand Canyon may release a sub-conscious prayer of wonder and awe. Similarly, an emergency will trigger a desperate cry to God for help. The prayer was there; it just needed to be released.

Even though we all inherently know how to pray simple prayers, we need instruction if these infrequent cries of the spirit are to mature into meaningful communication with God. The Scriptures are God's textbook on prayer. Here we meet the true object of our prayers, and in the pages of the Bible we learn the discipline of praying. The Bible is not a prerequisite to prayer, but it will perfect our praying.

Years ago, under my pastoral leadership, a congregation in Kennewick, Washington, USA, came into a vibrant prayer ministry. One of the results was a visitation of God that we called a spiritual awakening. As a result of the reports of what God was doing in our church, I was invited to hold a series of special services in the largest church in Eastern Washington. I was requested to teach this congregation some principles of prayer. After the first service, I told the pastor how impressed I was with the fervency of prayer exhibited by one young couple in the service.

'Yes,' he responded, 'they are very earnest and disciplined in their prayer but, quite frankly, it doesn't seem to accomplish much in their lives.'

'I don't understand that,' I said. 'If a person is disciplined to pray consistently, there certainly should be results.'

That week the pastor arranged for me to have some special prayer time with this couple to ferret out their difficulty. I found them to be extremely mystical, almost to the 'spooky' level, and their earnest and often dramatic prayers lacked sequence or substance. I had the feeling that, instead of going somewhere, we were flitting around like a kite with too short a tail.

I meditated on the situation that evening, and the next day I asked the young man about his Bible-reading habits.

'I really don't have time to read the Bible,' he confessed. 'I'm a student at the university, and my studies consume my reading time. I give myself to prayer. I leave it to others to read the Bible.'

'That's a dangerous imbalance,' I told him. 'May I earnestly urge you to divide your prayer time between devotionally reading the Bible and emotionally calling on God? You need to know better the God to whom you're praying, and you need to hear the Lord speak to you through his Word. You're conducting a monologue and calling it prayer.'

He proved to be teachable and accepted my suggestion. His pastor later reported to me that the prayer life of this young couple soon took on new meaning and power; the effects of their prayers could be sensed throughout the entire church. They, as we, merely needed some sound biblical instruction in prayer.

Frequently, we don't even know the difference between the urge to pray and the utterance of prayer. We get confused between the expression of a need and a petition for divine intervention in that need. But when we go to God's textbook, we begin to learn the nature of prayer, the purpose of prayer and the power of prayer.

Although it is true that many have learned how to pray by accident or by trial and error, having the Scriptures as a guide and the Holy Spirit as a teacher gives us a tremendous shortcut. The written Word – the Scriptures – and the living Word – Christ Jesus – introduce us to prayer and instruct us in our praying.

Prayer is a cry

Prayer, in its most elementary sense, is the cry of the inner person to something or someone considered higher than that person.

It is often an involuntary reaction that bypasses the conscious mind. Even non-religious people have been heard to exclaim, 'Oh, my God!' when something extraordinary has happened to them. Few people will leave this life without having uttered a prayer in one form or another, for built into the soul of every person is an awareness of God. When desperation overwhelms, prayer overtakes them.

Some people question the value of such desperate utterances of prayer but, over the years, I have repeatedly listened to testimonies of divine intervention that was viewed as an answer to a desperate cry. The mercy of Jehovah God is of such magnitude that I can believe he answers desperate cries flung out into the unknown. David said of God, 'The eyes of the Lord are on the righteous and his ears are attentive to their cry' (Psalm 34:15).

On one of my many flights across the USA, I was seated next to a gentleman considerably older than me. He wanted to talk, and, when he discovered that I was a minister, he insisted on telling me of his one 'religious experience'.

He had lived his life on the sea as a merchant seaman. Some years before, the ship on which he was working sank in the midst of a storm. Wearing a life-jacket and hanging on to a piece of flotsam, he was adrift in the sea. When the storm subsided, he saw nothing but open sea. Though he admitted that he lost track of time, he insisted that he drifted for several days. In desperation, he lifted his head towards the clear skies and cried, 'God, if there is a God, save me.'

He testified that within minutes he saw the silhouette of a ship on the horizon. It headed straight for him and rescued him. Although there was no indication of godliness in the behaviour of this man, he gave all the credit for his rescue to 'the Almighty God who watches out for seamen', as he put it. He didn't know the God to whom he prayed, nor did he understand the principles of prayer. In his desperation he called, and God answered.

This is prayer at its primitive level. The cry of an honest heart is heard by a holy God.

The experience of this seaman is consistent with the Scriptures. The psalmist wrote:

'[Some] went out on the sea in ships; they were merchants on the mighty waters. They saw the works of the Lord, his wonderful deeds in the deep. For he spoke and stirred up a tempest that lifted high the waves. They mounted up to the heavens and went down to the depths; in their peril their courage melted away. They reeled and staggered like drunken men; they were at their wits' end. Then they cried out to the Lord in their trouble, and he brought them out of their distress' (Psalm 107:23-28).

In seeking to help Job understand the reason for his misery, Elihu said of people: 'They plead for relief from the arm of the powerful' (Job 35:9). He also said of God, 'He heard the cry of the needy' (Job 34:28). There is a twofold reason for the cry of prayer. First, God is mighty; he is more than able to meet our need. Second, God is pledged to hear our cry.

The cry of prayer is a directed cry. It is a plea to one who is both able and willing to intervene in our affairs. It isn't like the plea for compassion a beggar may extend to a passer-by but more like the appeal of a son to his father for help in something that has become overwhelming. The cry of prayer is an authorised cry, and it is an honoured cry.

For the last three hundred years or so of their stay in Egypt, the Israelites were slaves to Pharaoh and his people. It is likely that this servitude was imposed a little at a time; had their liberties been removed in one quick action, it seems the Hebrews would have rebelled and overthrown Pharaoh. Human nature being what it is, liberty can be removed in small segments without threatening people's security. Eventually, however, these Hebrews were vassal slaves of the state system, and their lot became increasingly severe.

When conditions finally became intolerable, the people cried out to God for deliverance. In response to these cries, God called Moses into divine service at the burning bush and said, 'I have indeed seen the misery of my people in Egypt. I have heard them crying out because of their slave drivers, and I am concerned about their suffering. So I have come down to rescue them from the hand of the Egyptians' (Exodus 3:7-8).

Their cry got God's attention and released him to intervene in their misery. Their prayers may not have been very theological, and the praying people were dirty slaves rather than respectable ministers, but God heard their cries and answered their pleas.

Jesus told the parable of the unjust judge to show his disciples 'that they should always pray and not give up'. He summarised the message of the parable by saying, 'Will not God bring about justice for his chosen ones, who cry out to him day and night? Will he keep putting them off?' (Luke 18:1, 7).

The beginning level of prayer need not be anything more than a desperate cry to Almighty God. He will hear, and he will answer.

Prayer is a conversation

The Scriptures that assure us of God's response to our cries also show us that prayer is far more than emergency cries to an unseen force. Prayer is communication between people on the earth and God in heaven.

Whereas prayer as a *cry* is usually a monologue, prayer as *conversation* must be a dialogue. This higher form of prayer speaks to God and allows God to speak to us. It is the channel by which two separate worlds keep in contact with each other.

When the USA first landed astronauts on the surface of the moon, the whole world watched in awe. The technological miracle that put them on the moon was nearly dwarfed by the accompanying miracle of communication. We could see and hear them on television sets in our homes. There was almost instant communication between men on the moon and men in mission control. Although they were separated by more miles than have ever separated humans in the history of the world, the link of communication bridged that gap and united all action.

Prayer is like that. It links God with people. It bridges the gap between heaven and earth. It unites the actions of a holy God with his redeemed people. It enables us to be informed of God's designs, desires and deeds. It also enables God to offer us direction in our activities. It links mission control – heaven – with the spaceship earth.

In the Old Testament, communication between God and men or women often consisted of angels as the mediator that adapted heaven's frequencies to earthly channels. Angels acted as interpreters. In the New Testament, however, this is rarely seen. Jesus came to be that mediator, and he taught that all our prayer should be in his name. He said that our communication with the Father should be channelled through the Son.

The Scriptures abound with detailed illustrations of men and women who had conversations with God. Notable among them is the wife of Manoah to whom the angel of the Lord appeared and said, 'You are sterile and childless, but you are going to conceive and have a son.... The boy is to be a Nazirite, set apart to God from birth, and he will begin the deliverance of Israel from the hands of the Philistines' (Judges 13:3, 5).

When this woman reported the conversation to her husband, 'Manoah prayed to the Lord: "O Lord, I beg you, let the man of God you sent to us come again to teach us how to bring up the boy who is to be born." God heard Manoah, and the angel of God came again to the woman' (Judges 13:8-9).

When Manoah arrived on the scene, he carried on quite a conversation with this manifestation of God, asking questions and receiving answers. The questions were specific, and the answers were straightforward and understandable. The angel of the Lord was even willing to humour Manoah's request that he wait long enough for this couple to prepare a meal for him.

After this encounter, Samson was born. Neither the boy nor his ministry came as a surprise. The parents had held a lengthy conversation with God about all the details.

When we learn to let prayer be a two-way conversation with God, we discover that God is interested in far more than theology. He delights in discussing the everyday events of our lives. He is an expert in all areas of human experience. Surely, if he created everything, he must understand everything.

Perhaps the first genuine breakthrough people have in prayer is the discovery that they are simply talking to a loving God who has chosen to reveal himself as their Father in heaven. When we assimilate this truth, we are ready for the Bible to show us something even higher in prayer.

Prayer is communion

Genesis, the book of beginnings, indicates that, after the creation of humanity, God the Creator came into the Garden of Eden during the cool of the day to walk and talk with Adam, the creature. It was a time of fellowship and communion. God became the teacher, and Adam was an apt student.

What they talked about was far less important than the communion that transpired when they talked. Fundamentally, they were simply enjoying the company of each other. It was fellowship at its highest level. Adam desperately needed it and delightfully enjoyed it. This is the purest form of prayer – open, verbal communion and companionship with God. This fulfils the purpose of creation, and it ultimately satisfies the heart of the Creator. The Scriptures give us no indication whatever of how long this season of communion lasted, but we have every reason to believe that it was satisfying to God.

Eventually, sin broke this sweet fellowship. Adam and Eve were driven from the garden, and the personal, intimate companionship with God was replaced with the ritual of blood sacrifice. God is a holy God, and those who fellowship intimately with him must be holy people. It is bad enough that sin degrades and defiles us and eventually divorces us from the close personal relationship God has made available to his creatures.

As God has explained through the prophet, 'Your iniquities have separated you from your God' (Isaiah 59:2). Sin did not separate God from humankind, but it completely separated humankind from the fellowship of God. Sin killed humanity's relationship with God. This is why Paul got so excited by the substitutionary death of Jesus. He wrote: 'When you were dead in your sins . . . God made you alive with Christ. He forgave us all our sins' (Colossians 2:13).

We not only died with Christ at Calvary by identification; we have been made alive with Jesus Christ through identification with his resurrection. In the relationship with God, death has been superseded with life. John spoke similarly when he wrote, 'If we walk in the light, as he is in the light, we have fellowship with one another, and the blood of Jesus, his Son, purifies us from all sin' (1 John 1:7). In the context of this passage, the fellowship John refers to is fellowship with God.

Prayer, in its pristine form, is communion with God. Sin broke this communion, but the blood of Jesus Christ has restored it. Unfortunately many Christians feel that if they have been delivered from sin, they have automatically entered into the fulness of redemption. They fail to understand that Jesus did not come simply to remove sin from our lives. This is only a part of the process. He came to restore our fellowship with the Father. Removal of sin is a vital verity, but it is not the purpose of the process. Until we have been restored to the level of fellowship with God that Adam forfeited, the work of the cross is not yet complete in our lives.

Pure prayer is not manipulation of God; it is relationship with God. It goes far beyond asking and starts enjoying his presence. Prayer is talking to the Father, not simply because we are confused or confounded, but because we are lonely for him. David seemed to understand this, for he wrote:

'Give ear to my words, O Lord, consider my sighing. Listen to my cry for help, my King and my God, for to you I pray. O Lord, in the morning you hear my voice; in the morning I lay my requests before you and wait in expectation' (Psalm 5:1-3).

In another place he sang, 'My soul finds rest in God alone; my salvation comes from him. He alone is my rock and my salvation' (Psalm 62:1-2). David often petitioned God, but he stated that his primary purpose for prayer was to restore fellowship with the God he so deeply loved.

Even a casual reader of the Bible would know that Moses was a praying man. The one thing that makes him stand out above many other praying people in the Scriptures is that 'the Lord would speak to Moses face to face, as a man speaks with his friend' (Exodus 33:11). Moses and God were far more than working partners in getting the Hebrew people from Egypt to the promised land. God and Moses developed an intimate friendship. When Moses prayed, he entered into the fellowship and communion that exists between close friends. Was this rare relationship available only to this great giver of the Law?

Jesus told his disciples and, by implication, told us: 'You are my friends if you do what I command. I no longer call you servants, because a servant does not his master's business. Instead, I have called you

22

friends, for everything I learned from my Father I have made known to you' (John 15:14-15). The God-man, Christ Jesus, has made available to us the same friendly relationship that Moses enjoyed with God.

If it were not for the Scriptures, it is likely that our prayers would never ascend beyond desperate cries. It is as we read God's Word and dare to accept his provision for our lives and claim his redemption that we can communicate with God and enter into a friendly relationship that makes communion with God an everyday event.

Aside from the Bible, all attempts to find this relationship are doomed to failure. The human heart is wicked and deceitful. Our depraved minds constantly accuse us to ourselves. The depravity of our human nature causes us to flee *from* God rather than flee *to* him. It isn't until we say about ourselves what the Scriptures say about us that we dare come into God's presence on friendly terms. We would never know the power of confession, except that the Bible says to confess our sins. We couldn't experience the joy of forgiveness apart from the promise of the Scriptures. We earthbound creatures would never have known that we were children of God if God hadn't declared it in his Word.

The desperate cry of prayer may not need much Scripture to shape and mold it, but the ascending levels of prayer, which eventually bring us into intimate fellowship with God, depend wholly on the Bible. When my heart accuses me and thereby cuts off my prayer fellowship with God, I turn to the portions of God's Book that speak assurance of forgiveness and pray them aloud. Seeing them, saying them and then hearing myself declare what God has declared about me lifts me from fear to faith and from despondency to dependency.

We can have fellowship and communion with God in prayer, not because we desire it but because he has declared it. I don't have to produce it, for God has already provided it through Christ Jesus. I need only to embrace it, express it and enjoy it. Prayer is the best channel through which this glorious provision of the Bible is released.

The most casual reader of the Bible cannot escape being introduced to prayer, for the book is full of prayers, praying people and the divine intervention that prayer produces. When the awesome power of prayer grips our attention, we notice that the same Bible invites us to become praying people. Prayer isn't restricted to special people. To all who will listen, God says, 'Call to me and I will answer you and tell you great and unsearchable things you do not know' (Jeremiah 33:3).

2

Praying the Scriptures invites us to pray

'Pastor, will you please pray for me? The rent's due, and I don't have enough money to pay it.'

Thousands of times I had previously responded to similar requests from the sheep of my flock. They expressed great confidence in my contact with God, and I found myself in the role of intercessor and, sometimes, mediator. This request was especially pathetic, as this woman had been badly abused by her alcoholic husband who was in jail for theft. She was the sole support of a large family. Lacking any job skills, she took whatever work she could find as a cleaner. In our church she had experienced a precious encounter with the Lord a few months prior to this request, and she responded quickly to the ministry of the church.

Opening my mouth to promise to take her need to the Father in my morning prayer time, I was amazed to hear what I said to her. 'Sister, why don't you ask God to meet this need?'

'But, pastor,' she responded, 'I can't pray. I'm just a new convert, and I don't know the Bible as you do.'

Sensing that the Spirit wanted to expand her spiritual walk, I explained, 'Answered prayer is never keyed to the position of the person who prays; it is vested in the provision of God. God doesn't answer my prayers because I'm a pastor but because he's promised to answer prayer. Jesus said, 'If you remain in me and my words remain in you, ask whatever you wish, and it will be given you' [John 15:7]. Go into the prayer room and talk to Jesus just as you talk to me. Inform him that the rent is due, and that you need additional money. Tell him exactly how much money you need.'

I'll never know what thoughts went through her mind as she obediently headed for the prayer room. I've always suspected that she thought I was rejecting her and withdrawing myself from any responsibility to meet her need. I slipped into my study and asked the Lord to meet this new convert at the point of her need.

On Thursday night she came to church with the first big smile I had ever seen on her face. During the sharing time she told about being pressed to pray for herself and how insufficient she felt in such urgent praying. But, she reported, God had answered. In a most unusual way, from a source totally removed from the church, she had received the exact amount she had prayed for.

As the woman gave her glowing testimony, the Spirit spoke to me and said, 'See, son, it is better to teach them to pray than always to do their praying for them.'

In the months that followed, this sister became a faithful prayer warrior who regularly lifted her pastor before the throne of grace in prayer. She matured from a person who depended on others to pray to one on whom others could depend for prayer. She found her privilege as a child of God, and she learned to enjoy answering God's invitation to pray.

The Scriptures extend an invitation to pray

This same principle is seen in the Bible. When young Samuel was awakened by hearing someone call his name, he responded immediately to Eli, the priest, who said, 'I did not call; go back and lie down' (1 Samuel 3:6).

When this happened a second time, 'Eli told Samuel, "Go and lie down, and if he calls you, say, 'Speak, Lord, for your servant is listening' " ' (1 Samuel 3:9). Samuel obeyed, and when God again called his name, 'Samuel said, "Speak, for your servant is listening" ' (1 Samuel 3:10).

Samuel's response released God to tell what he purposed to do with the house of Eli. From this encounter came the commission that placed Samuel, a young servant to Eli, into the office of a prophet, one who also functioned as a priest and a judge in Israel. The Scripture says, 'The Lord was with Samuel as he grew up, and he let none of his words fall to the ground' (1 Samuel 3:19).

All of this came to pass because Samuel accepted God's invitation to pray. God initiated the conversation, but at first Samuel felt that divine communication would come only to those holding divine offices; God couldn't be speaking to a young boy. But Eli, for all of his failures, was wise enough to realise that God wants to communicate with anyone who has a listening ear.

Have you ever had that inner sense of God's presence but did not respond? We often treat carelessly a divine call to prayer. Similarly, we read the Scriptures and see the repeated invitations to call upon the Lord, but we read right on without responding. God initiates prayer by extending this invitation to communicate with himself. But unless we respond, it will remain only an invitation.

Occasionally, when I realised that I was being beckoned into God's presence through prayer but did not feel worthy or 'in the mood' to pray, I prayed God's invitation: 'Go, my people, enter your rooms and shut the doors behind you; hide yourselves for a little while until his wrath has passed by. See, the Lord is coming out of his dwelling' (Isaiah 26:20-21).

Simply reading that aloud and adding, 'Lord, I come,' has often bridged the gap between my reticence and his readiness for prayer. The Scriptures gave me the message and the motive. They helped me to desire what God desired: communion.

Divine invitation, not human desperation, should be the motivation for prayer. Prayer is not a last resort; it is our first resource. Paul instructed the Christians in Philippi, 'Do not be anxious about anything, but in everything, by prayer and petition, with thanksgiving, present your requests to God' (Philippians 4:6). In these few words, Paul introduces God's *plan* for prayer, his *panorama* of prayer, the *pattern* of prayer and the *performance* of prayer. God's invitation to pray is very explicit and inclusive.

The invitation contains an explanation

Whether we view this as an invitation, a proclamation or a mandate, God is explaining that his *plan* for handling anxiety in human nature is prayer. Anxiety is destructive. It saps energy, restricts our thinking, limits our joy and hinders our relationship with God.

Our heavenly Father says, 'Humble yourselves...under God's mighty hand, that he may lift you up in due time. Cast all your anxiety on him because he cares for you' (1 Peter 5:6-7). Human pride causes us to continue to wrestle with our anxieties, but when we humble ourselves enough to ask help from God, he reveals his plan for lifting our load.

The *panorama* of God's provision in prayer is staggering. There is absolutely nothing in the realm of our anxieties that should be withheld from God. 'Do not be anxious about anything, but in everything, by prayer,' Paul stated. Listening to the theological treatises that are given as prayers in some churches would cause us to believe that God is interested only in theology. Actually, God is interested in life. He is life, he has given life and he is the preserver of life. Nothing will ever come into our lives that cannot be discussed with God in prayer.

Paul also assured all Christians, 'I am convinced that neither death nor life, neither angels nor demons, neither the present nor the future, nor any powers, neither height nor depth, nor anything else in all creation, will be able to separate us from the love of God that is in Christ Jesus our Lord' (Romans 8:38-39).

What an invitation prayer is to the believer! Its panorama covers the past, the present and the future. It covers the heavens above and the earth below. It affects the divine realm, the human realm and even the demonic realm. Every need and situation in every realm, in every period of time, can be brought to God in prayer. The scope of this invitation is staggering.

The *pattern* for responding to this elaborate invitation is 'by prayer and supplication'. The Old Testament order was sacrifice and offerings, but the New Testament pattern of approach to God is 'prayer and supplication'. God is simply saying, 'Let's talk it over.' We need not make propitiation, for he 'sent his Son as an atoning sacrifice for our sins' (1 John 4:10).

God is not even demanding an offering from us before he will show an interest in our worries. 'We have been made holy through the sacrifice of the body of Jesus Christ once for all' (Hebrews 10:10). We are invited to come empty-handed to unload all our cares on him.

An unknown author once penned:

It is his will that I should cast
My care on him each day.
He also bids me not to cast
My confidence away.
But oh! how foolishly I act,
When taken unaware.
I cast away my confidence,
And carry all my care.

Like the husband who buys the expensive gift for his wife, only to discover what she really wanted was for him to talk to her, we often do the 'big' thing for God when he merely wanted to have a conversation with us. He invites us to pray – not to pay. He asks for our supplication rather than our service. He wants to have fellowship with his saints, and prayer is the beginning channel for that companionship.

In Philippians 4:6, Paul adds that the *performance* of prayer must include thanksgiving. It is likely that experience had taught Paul that dealing exclusively with anxieties, fears and problems can lead to discouragement and depression. Along with the expression of our worries, we need to express our thanksgiving for God's nature, his promises and his prior intervention into our affairs.

When God gave Samuel and the men of Israel a stunning victory over the invading Philistines, 'Samuel took a stone and set it up between Mizpah and Shen. He named it Ebenezer, saying, "Thus far has the Lord helped us" ' (1 Samuel 7:12).

Believers need to erect an Ebenezer stone at every point of victory in their lives. The next time they are threatened, they can look back and say, 'Thus far has the Lord helped us.'

When we tell God 'Thank you' for what he has done or for who he has revealed himself to be to us, the door opens to heartfelt supplication for further help. Someone who continues to petition without expressing thanks and praise reveals an arrogant attitude of deserving.

When in prayer, if you cannot think of anything to thank God for, do what I regularly do: Thank God that you haven't received from him what you really deserve!

Sometimes dinner invitations add 'black tie requested', so that guests know that formal dress is expected. If you comply you will not be embarrassed on arrival. Similarly, God's invitation to pray includes the notation that response is 'with thanksgiving'. All who enter the realm of prayer without thanksgiving will be out of place and will be chagrined and ashamed. The psalmist reminds us always to wear the garment of thanksgiving when entering the courts of prayer and praise: 'Enter his gates with thanksgiving and his courts with praise; give thanks to him and praise his name' (Psalm 100:4).

The invitation comes with an RSVP

If you have ever hosted a major event, you know how difficult it is to plan until you have some indication of how many people will accept the invitation to attend. Banquets have been nearly ruined when far more people showed up than were expected. Conversely, facilities seating thousands have been rented for an evening and remained embarrassingly empty.

How well I remember being invited to Albuquerque, New Mexico, to speak at a convention. The sponsors were excited to have succeeded in leasing the civic auditorium, seating thousands of people. But less than a hundred people showed up. We rattled around in that huge hall for two days. A cafeteria would have been more cosy.

To avoid such waste and embarrassment many invitations include an RSVP, which is an abbreviation for the French version of 'please reply'. For many such occasions, no provision is made for people who don't respond. Common courtesy calls for letting the host or hostess know whether or not you will be able or willing to attend.

The scriptural invitation to pray also contains an RSVP. God's invitation requests an indication of our acceptance or rejection. While it is easy to establish a biblical mandate for prayer, Scripture doesn't say that God demands that we pray. He entices us to pray; he often puts us in situations where it is expedient that we pray, but we are not compelled to pray as much as we are invited to pray. God desires it, but he doesn't demand it.

Sometimes we respond to this invitation with joy and gladness, but at other times we need the strong promptings of others. When Jonah finally obeyed God and delivered the message of God's impending wrath upon Nineveh, the king of Nineveh issued a proclamation in Nineveh, saying, "Do not let any man or beast, herd or flock, taste anything; do not let them eat or drink. But let man and beast be covered with sackcloth. Let everyone *call urgently on God.* Let them give up their evil ways and their violence. Who knows? God may yet relent and with compassion turn from his fierce anger so that we will not perish.' When God saw what they did and how they turned from their evil ways, he had compassion and did not bring upon them the destruction he had threatened' (Jonah 3:7-10).

Obedience to the instruction of this earthly king brought the mercy of God upon the people. Would not an honest response to the King of kings bring an even greater demonstration of divine grace and mercy upon his people?

It is painful to admit that there have been times

when I so wanted my own way that I refused to pray. I stumbled in my walk, fumbled in my talk and offered a ministry of human energy instead of divine provision. I pleaded business and distraction, but the truth was simply that I was rejecting God's invitation to communicate with him. When I finally bent my will and went to him in prayer, my soul was bathed clean of its defilement, my spirit was renewed in God's life, and the dark cloud of frustration was dispelled with the bright light of God's presence. Joseph Scriven knew well what he was saying when he wrote:

O what peace we often forfeit,
O what needless pain we bear,
All because we do not carry
Everything to God in prayer.

In the last teaching session Jesus had with his disciples before his arrest and crucifixion, he said, 'You may ask me for anything in my name, and I will do it' (John 14:14). In essence, he was saying, 'Respond to the invitation and rejoice in the benefits.'

The power of prayer is found in its performance, not in its provision. Provisionally God has already met our needs, for he has revealed himself to be *Jehovah-jireh* – the Lord who provides. This provision is subject to our request. God offers to meet our needs RSVP. James told the saints, 'You want something but don't get it. You kill and covet, but you cannot have what you want. You quarrel and fight. You do not have, because you do not ask God' (James 4:2). What we cannot produce through our own efforts, God has already provided, and he has invited us to enter into that provision through prayer. We need only to pray the cry of David, 'I am poor and needy.... Help me, O Lord my God.... Let them know that this is your hand, that you, O Lord, have done it' (Psalm 109:22, 26-27). This is a marvellous response to God's invitation to help.

Prayer is an activity. It is not a spectator sport. Listening to another pray is not prayer. Commiserating with your misery is not prayer, either. Prayer demands participation in communicating with God. It demands involvement, and the Scriptures marvellously involve us in prayer.

3

Praying the Scriptures involves us in prayer

He was a PK – a preacher's kid – who had left home, married and abandoned the early training he had received in the vicarage. A crisis in his marriage caused him to seek out a church for solace. After the sermon he responded to the altar call I issued, and there he knelt in absolute silence. I tried to help him cry out to God, but to everything I said he countered, 'I know that, but I have no peace in my heart. I'm lost.'

Laying hands on him, I prayed one of my finer theological prayers fully expecting him to respond joyfully to my proclamation of God's saving grace. His response was unemotional, as if I had given him a stock quotation. Realising that he had not in any way identified with my prayer, I asked him to pray a prayer of repentance and to ask Christ Jesus to become his Lord.

'I can't pray,' was his only response. 'I've tried for weeks, but no prayer will come out.'

'Then pray after me,' I said.

Laboriously, he mimicked the words I spoke, but it was obvious that they didn't come from his heart, nor did they ascend much above his head. Desperate to reach him, I opened the Bible to 1 John 1:9 and said, 'Pray this.'

He read the verse silently and simply remarked, 'I learned this in Sunday school years ago.'

'Then pray it!' I commanded. 'Cry it to God as a desperate man cries, 'Help!' when he realises that he's drowning.'

Rather quietly, he recited the verse, 'If we confess our sins, he is faithful and just and will forgive us our sins and purify us from all unrighteousness.'

'That's a promise,' I said. 'Plead it before God's throne.'

Again and again he recited this verse until his soul laid hold of it as a prayer. He ceased leaning across the altar, and he stretched himself upright on his knees. With head lifted towards heaven, he began to pray, 'Thank God, since I've confessed my sins, he has faithfully and justly forgiven me all my sins. I've been cleansed from all unrighteousness.'

Joy magnified in his heart. He began to praise the Lord like a seasoned saint. The fruit of his life in the years that followed proved that he had prayed from an honest heart to a holy God; God had met him and answered his cry.

The change came when I involved him in prayer by having him say back to God what God had said to him in the Scriptures. 'Faith comes from hearing the message, and the message is heard through the word of Christ,' Paul assures us in Romans 10:17. When we pray the pure Word of God, we open ourselves to pure faith, and we cannot help but get involved in pure prayer.

Praying the Scriptures leads us to simplicity

One of this young man's problems was that his approach to God was much too complex. His difficulty is common. We live in a complex age, and it is hard for us to approach God in simplicity. After all, we are the generation that put men on the moon. We are surrounded with the miracles of colour television and aeroplanes. Our lives are so complex that we can hardly handle them.

Many years ago, E.M. Bounds, a great man of prayer, wrote: 'Men prayed in Old Testament times because they were simple men who lived in simple times. They were childlike, lived in childlike times and had childlike faith' *(Prayer and Praying Men)*. The simplicity of the lives these people lived made prayer as natural as sowing and reaping or marriage and family.

As I've travelled and ministered in what are called developing countries, I have found prayer far more vibrant and natural than it is in the West. Those Christians tend to exhibit a simple trust in God's provision and a genuine enjoyment of his person. They have few other things to distract their thoughts away from God, and they live in a necessary dependence on him. We often look to our governmental agencies or to the business sector to meet needs. They cry out to God. Prayer becomes as natural as breathing when God is the only resource available.

We might wish we could return to such simplicity of life, but it is improbable that civilisation would willingly step backwards in its standard of living. We have our accepted substitutes for God, both in the state and in the church, and it is difficult to tear down adored idols.

Simply put, complexity wars against prayer. There is a prevailing sense that, if we put our minds to it, we can solve the difficulty, meet the need, find satisfaction in things or activities rather than in God himself.

Jesus told his disciples, 'Children, how hard it is to for those who trust in riches to enter the kingdom of God! It is easier for a camel to go through the eye of a needle than for a rich man to enter the kingdom of God' (Mark 10:24-25 RAV). This is not Christ's condemnation of wealth or a declaration that possession of things keeps us out of the kingdom. What he declared was that *dependence* on riches virtually negates dependence on God. How often the almighty God has been replaced with the almighty dollar or pound.

Finding our security outside of relationship with God is the American and European way of life. 'Be self-sufficient,' we hear from our childhood, and therefore we reserve prayer for extreme emergencies. Prayer is the fire-escape of life; we want it handy if everything goes up in smoke.

When we pray, as the Scriptures teach us to pray, we learn that prayer is a relationship of dependence. It is a child communicating with his or her heavenly Father. Jesus set a little child in the midst of his disciples and said, 'I tell you the truth, unless you change and become like little children, you will never enter the kingdom of heaven. Therefore, whoever humbles himself like this child is the greatest in the kingdom of heaven' (Matthew 18:3-4).

This may sound super-simple, but implementing it is intricately involved. It demands a one-hundred-and-eighty-degree *change of direction* ('change'), *humility* ('humbles himself'), *dependency* ('like this child') and *loss of rights,* for children do not have the same rights as adults. They live in the rights conferred upon them by their parents.

These are the attitudes we see exemplified in the lives of praying men and women in the Scriptures, and these are the attitudes devotional Bible reading will produce in praying people today. We are but children of God. His knowledge is superior to ours. His provision is our only source of life. We live in complete dependence on him. All prayer must flow out of these concepts.

Reading the Scriptures makes us aware that prayer is asking and receiving. It is like sitting at a family meal and asking, 'Please pass the potatoes.' No pleading is necessary. The provision was made when the potatoes were put on the table. Our asking is merely a way of making another aware that we desire some of the provision. Prayer is asking for God's provision to be passed to our place. Our parents have provided it, cooked it and placed it on the table. Now we gently request that our portion be passed down the table to us. How different this is from the hopeless praying that I have witnessed in watching idol worshippers throughout the world!

When God appeared to young King Solomon and said, 'Ask for whatever you want me to give you,' Solomon responded, 'I am only a little child and do not know how to carry out my duties' (1 Kings 3:5, 7). He wasn't referring to his chronological age, for he was a married king over Israel, nor was he expressing false humility. When Solomon compared himself with his father, David, and viewed the tremendous task that lay before him, he felt totally insufficient for the job. He took the position of a child before Father God, and this greatly pleased the Lord, who endowed Solomon with great wisdom.

The more we use the Scriptures in our time of prayer, the greater depth of humility we will attain; our consciousness of dependency upon a loving Father's care will increase with every prayer. We cannot return to the simple life on the farm, but we must maintain a simple childlike dependency upon God.

Praying the Scriptures brings us to sincerity

Our English word *sincere* comes from two Greek words: *sine*, 'without', and *cere*, 'wax'. The word was a merchant's term coined in the days of Paul. The silver merchants habitually covered imperfections and flaws in their merchandise with beeswax impregnated with silver filings. The piece looked perfect, but the first time heat was applied, the wax melted and ran, leaving the imperfection glaringly visible.

Fully knowing the meaning of the word, Paul wrote, 'This I pray...that you may approve the things that are excellent, that you may be sincere and without offence till the day of Christ' (Philippians 1:9-10 RAV). He prayed that the saints would be free from fraud, deceit and misconduct until Jesus returned. This, of course, should be the goal of every Christian believer. We need to be 'no-wax' Christians.

If there is one place where insincerity is manifested in Christian behaviour, it is apt to be in prayer. Especially public prayer. I have often cringed while listening to a public prayer in a congregational gathering. What was being said was far from what was in the heart and life of the person offering the prayer. It sounded good, and it was probably what the people wanted to hear, but it was not an honest expression of the person's life.

I remember hearing a leader earnestly beseech God for purity in the church when I knew that he was having an affair with his secretary. In another instance, I pastored a church under great financial pressure. I heard a miserly member, who refused to pay tithes and seldom put more than a dollar in the offering, express a nearly eloquent prayer pleading with God to supply the need.

Whom do we think we are kidding? If there is deception, it is self-deception. God knows our hearts, our minds and our motivations. The warmth of his presence soon melts the deceitful wax and exposes the flaws in our character.

Insincere prayer is often an attempt to look better than we really are. But those who use the Scriptures in their prayers are very aware of who they are and rejoice that God loves them anyway. They need not parade their hypothetical goodness. They have learned to live in the goodness of God.

In the Sermon on the Mount, Jesus taught, 'When you pray, do not be like the hypocrites, for they love to stand praying in the synagogues and on the street corners to be seen by men. I tell you the truth, they have received their reward in full' (Matthew 6:5). This is not an indictment against public praying; it is a condemnation of insincerity in prayer. It was illustrated by Jesus a little later in his ministry when he told this parable:

'Two men went up to the temple to pray, one a Pharisee and the other a tax collector. The Pharisee stood up and prayed about himself: "God, I thank you that I am not like all other men – robbers, evil-doers, adulterers – or even like this tax collector. I fast twice a week and give a tenth of all I get." But the tax collector stood at a distance. He would not even look up to heaven, but beat his breast and said, "God, have mercy on me, a sinner." I tell you that this man, rather than the other, went home justified before God' (Luke 18:10-14).

The prayer that has a direct connection to heaven is prayer that comes from a sincere heart. It may lack eloquence, and it may even be theologically suspect, but if it is honest to the heart and life of the one praying, God will listen and respond.

I have been reared in a religious culture that places a high value on extemporaneous public praying. We don't use a prayer book. I have learned that sincere cries from the human heart excite God. Sometimes they are akin to a baby's cry of pain; at other times they sound like a child enjoying a new toy. Many times my spirit has leaped in excitement as I have listened to God's children pour out their hearts before him.

Sometimes the joy of the Lord can be expressed

only in laughter; at other times, his presence melts us to tears. Some prayers we whisper; others we shout – but God doesn't measure the value of the prayer by its form of expression. Great and powerful prayers simply come from the honest sincerity of heart and life. Jesus said, 'God is spirit, and his worshippers must worship in spirit and in *truth*' (John 4:24).

Praying the Scriptures gets us involved

Westerners have become spectators of life more than participants in life. We observe sports; we watch entertainment. We play music cassettes or discs rather than a musical instrument. We are so accustomed to paying to have almost everything done for us that we have virtually forgotten how to do much of anything outside of our job-related activities.

We bring this cultural attitude with us to church. Many sit with a mental remote control and switch from channel to channel during the church service. They tune in and out according to what satisfies them at the moment. They may, or may not, join in the singing, and as for public prayer, they rarely add more than an 'Amen!' to the end of someone else's prayer.

Even those few brave souls who attend the weekly 'prayer meeting' often find themselves non-participant listeners of the prayers of others. It isn't that they can't pray or even that they won't pray. They simply need something to get them going.

Quoting, or reading, the pure Word of God *breaks the inertia*. As a pastor, I faced this inertia on regular occasions. Sometimes I could 'prime the pump' with my prayer. But at other times the competition merely said the final 'Amen!' Otherwise they sat quietly. Occasionally, before the service, I would prepare portions of Scripture on slips of paper and hand them to individuals as they arrived. During the prayer time, I would call for that verse to be read, and then I would ask the entire congregation to pray this verse audibly. More often than not, the person who had publicly read the verse felt released to pray further, beyond merely quoting the Bible passage.

Praying the Scriptures will also *express deep emotion*. Many of us are locked up emotionally. We have difficulty getting in touch with our true feelings, and it is laborious to put those feelings into words. Believing that public expression of tenderness is evidence of weakness, we actually bite our lips to repress tears or laughter. Because of this, our prayers often lack pathos and feeling. We recite them like the register at school – accurately, but without feeling. No salesman could put bread on his table if he used that approach to selling. Effective communication has feeling in it, and God deserves to hear affectionate and passionate talk.

Just as some salesmen have developed a presentation that is as plastic as a bin-liner, so some Christians have developed an unnatural pitch of voice, choice of words and tenor of expression when they pray. Why do we have to talk to God differently from how we talk to other people? We don't possess separate spiritual emotions and natural emotions. We have but one set of emotions, which cover both our souls and our spirits.

When God challenged me to respond to him in praise and worship, I found that I could comfortably respond emotionally to God only as I played the organ. The music was my praise. But God told me to stay off the organ stool – not even to turn on an organ without his permission. I now know that he was forcing me to release my emotions towards him with words.

At the time, I had to respond with blind obedience. I would go to the church early in the morning, pick up my Bible and walk up and down the centre aisle of the auditorium reading portions of the psalms to God: 'To you, O Lord, I lift up my soul; in you I trust, O my God' (Psalm 25:1). Then I would make the verse my prayer. Sometimes I needed only one verse; other days, I would use an entire psalm. I discovered that every emotion in the human soul is released in the book of Psalms; reading them prayerfully until they became my prayer triggered a release in my own spirit.

We can't pray the Scriptures without *getting involved* in praying. Just as it breaks the inertia and gets us going and expresses deep emotion that gets us feeling, praying the Scriptures also puts thoughts into words and gets us talking. There is power in God's Word to get us praying. When we say back to God what he has said to us, we are already in communication with him. From there, it is an easy step to move the conversation to what is on our hearts.

There is no more useful tool to get us into prayer than God's precious Word. If we will read it, pray it and practice it, the Word will motivate us into prayer. As we use the Scriptures to aid our praying, we will discover them to be God's chosen textbook on prayer. Praying the Scriptures instructs us in prayer that is pleasing to God, productive for us and powerful in its outreach.

4

Praying the Scriptures instructs us in prayer

How often I have wished I could have been one of the twelve disciples who travelled with Jesus and learned from his ministry.

What a privilege to listen to him teach with an authority never before known! How startled the disciples must have been to see Christ cure the lepers, open blind eyes, cause the deaf to hear. Jesus' power and authority over death must have amazed these men as they watched the dead respond to his commands: the young boy sit up in his coffin, the young lady rise off her death bed, Lazarus walk out of his tomb days after he had been buried.

In teaching these disciples, Jesus said, 'I tell you the truth, anyone who has faith in me will do what I have been doing. He will do even greater things than these, because I am going to the Father' (John 14:12). Just imagine their response to this: What they had witnessed Jesus doing would be done by them. Still, we never read of their requesting to learn how to teach, preach, heal the sick or raise the dead.

What did they request? 'Lord, teach us to pray' (Luke 11:1). Either they coveted the authority and intimacy they sensed in Jesus' prayer life, or they recognised that his prayer life was the fountain from which all other ministry flowed. They wanted to relate to the heavenly Father as the Son on earth related to him. They were wise enough to 'eagerly desire the greater gifts' (1 Corinthians 12:31). May God grant that same desire to the disciples of this century.

The Scriptures instruct us *to* pray

Although Jesus granted their request and taught them to pray, he later had to instruct his disciples, 'Watch and pray so that you will not fall into temptation' (Mark 14:38). Knowing how to pray wasn't enough. They had to *do* it. Quite obviously, merely remaining, or remaining alert, was insufficient. They needed to touch the Father through the prayer channel.

Paul learned this secret, and he wrote, 'Pray continually' (1 Thessalonians 5:17).

Prayer should be as natural to Christian living as walking or breathing, but it is far too often reserved for emergencies or special occasions.

At other times we mistake anxiety and worry for prayer. This was true of a young husband who came to me for counsel.

He was obviously troubled. He was neglecting his physical appearance, and his nervous hand-gestures spoke of deep emotional distress. At first he answered my exploratory questions in one-syllable words, but when the emotional dam burst, he poured out his marital problems non-stop. I could feel his hurt, and I appreciated his deep yearning for healing of the marriage. I knew, however, that if he kept repressing his feelings, he would do himself emotional harm.

'Have you tried praying about this?' I asked.

'I've prayed about it day and night for over a week,' he replied.

'Let me blend my faith with yours as I join you in your prayer,' I said. 'Lift your voice and cry to God.'

Slipping out of my chair and pushing it back from the desk, I got on my knees. He followed my example, but silence descended on the room like a thick fog coming in from the sea. To break the silence, I offered a prayer on his behalf, but he didn't even say an amen. Silence again reigned, so I prompted him, 'You lead out in prayer.'

'I can't pray,' he said.

No amount of coaching or urging could coax a word out of this distraught brother. I went over to the man, put my hand on his shoulder and said, 'Brother, you haven't been praying about this problem day and night for a week, or you would be able to express your need in prayer to God here in my study. You have been worrying and thinking about your problem consistently, but that isn't prayer.'

Turning to the Psalms, I had him read aloud: 'Hear, O Lord, my righteous plea; listen to my cry. Give ear to my prayer – it does not rise from deceitful lips. May my vindication come from you; may your eyes see what is right' (Psalm 17:1-2). Slowly he made this psalm his prayer, and he moved from worry to prayer. When he put his anxiety into words, a great release came, making it possible to talk sensibly about the problem. And it was praying the Scriptures that gave him those words to speak.

Far too many Christians confuse thought with prayer. Because of my itinerant ministry, I spend many days away from home. When I phone my wife in the evening, it is useless to say, 'I've been talking to you all day.' She knows better than that. She would rather hear, 'I've been thinking about you all day,' for that is closer to the truth. It is wise to think before we speak, but it is dishonest to equate thinking with communicating. Thoughts are not prayers until they are expressed. It is scriptural for us to meditate on the Lord, but it is equally scriptural for us to express our innermost thoughts to God in prayer.

It is positive and proper for us to formulate prayers in our minds and to express them audibly to God. The psalmist sang: 'I cried out to him with my mouth; his praise was on my tongue.... God has surely listened and heard my voice in prayer. Praise be to God, who has not rejected my prayer or withheld his love from me!' (Psalm 66:17, 19-20). God wants to hear what is on our minds.

Prayer is more than a thought; it is communication of that thought. It goes beyond an attitude and becomes an attitude expressed. When we vocally bring the Scriptures into our prayers, we move beyond mere reflection on God to honest response to God. We move from pondering to praying.

Jesus taught his disciples that there was a *definiteness of purpose* in prayer. Having warned them against the hypocrisy of public display of prayers, he said: 'When you pray, go into your room, close the door and pray to your Father, who is unseen. Then your Father, who sees what is done in secret, will reward you' (Matthew 6:6).

In these few words, Jesus gave at least five specifics about praying. He established, first, that prayer involved a *period of time* – 'when you pray'. We never have time for prayer; we have to make time in our daily schedule. Although the morning hours are usually considered the best time for prayer since the first part of the day sets the tone for the remainder, there is nothing spiritual about morning prayer. David said, 'Evening, morning and noon I cry out in distress, and he hears my voice' (Psalm 55:17). It is not the time that is set, but the setting of a time for which Christ calls; unscheduled prayer is always acceptable, but a schedule for prayer is Christ's command.

Jesus also suggested that there be a *place* for

prayer – 'your room'. It is easier for us to institute the habit of prayer if we have an established place for prayer. For many years I have reserved a certain chair in my office for prayer. When at my desk I seem to get distracted from prayer, but when I kneel or sit in my 'prayer chair', my habit patterns make me conscious that this is prayer time.

Jesus retired regularly to a garden for prayer, and the prophet Habakkuk had his 'watch-tower'. Our 'room' may be a bedroom, a corner of the living-room or any other specific place, but we all need a place where we regularly return for prayer. As a pastor, I always set aside in the church a prayer room, reserved exclusively for prayer. Just walking into the room set church members in an attitude of prayer.

Jesus taught a third definite factor in praying: the *need for privacy* – 'close the door'. We must learn to pray to our Father 'in secret'. Most public praying would be more vital if it had been preceded with secret praying. Time after time I've noticed that men and women who have been mightily used of God have been those who have learned to spend private time with God.

A fourth factor in praying is to *know the person* to whom we pray – 'your Father, who sees what is done in secret'. Prayer is not scriptural prayer unless it is addressed to God. In the model prayer, Jesus said, 'This...is how you should pray: "Our Father in heaven" ' (Matthew 6:9). Prayer is communication to a known individual. He is 'our Father'. The better we know him, the easier prayer will be.

Jesus' fifth factor in prayer is the *promise of an open blessing* – the Father 'will reward you'. Prayer is never a one-way conversation. When we pray to the Father in secret, he answers us openly.

It is highly unlikely that we would ever understand such definiteness of purpose in prayer except through the revelation of the Word of God. The more we mix the Scriptures with our prayer, the more we will pray in the will of God and according to the pattern of God. No-one made prayer work for him better than Jesus, and it is he who instructs us to have a definite time, place, privacy, person to pray to and expectation of a divine response.

The Scriptures instruct us *how* to pray

My homiletics instructor in college was so predictable he was boring. His greeting was unvaried; his order of presentation was consistent; his style of communication lacked enthusiasm. We students were weary before he began.

I hear that boring sameness in much praying. It never varies; it repeats the same phrases; and it is void of any emotion. The Scriptures, when introduced into our prayers, help cure this rote response. They teach us the *diversity of performance* that keeps prayers interesting.

The epistle of Jude urges us: 'You, dear friends, build yourselves up in your most holy faith and pray in the Holy Spirit. Keep yourselves in God's love' (Jude 20-21). What infinite variety 'praying in the Holy Spirit' can bring to a prayer time!

As Paul wrote: 'We do not know what we ought to pray for, but the Spirit himself intercedes for us with groans that words cannot express' (Romans 8:26). We lack not only the proper concepts for which to pray; we lack the proper words with which to express those concerns.

The resident Spirit of God in the life of the believer knows the needs of the church; he knows the mind and will of God; and he knows how to express prayer through the lips of the believer. It is quite unimportant whether he expresses prayer through a believer in that person's native tongue or bypasses the prayer's conscious mind to express the higher purposes of God without the restrictions of human censorship. What is so vital is this: God within us is communicating with God above us, and we know that this communication is pure and powerful.

Paul addressed this form of prayer in a letter to the Christians in Corinth: 'If I pray in a tongue, my spirit prays, but my mind is unfruitful. So what shall I do? I will pray with my spirit, but I will also pray with my mind' (1 Corinthians 14:14-15).

The various psalmists reveal different modes of praying to God. They speak of singing prayer, shouting prayer, weeping in prayer, united prayer and private prayer. They used different methods of expressing those prayers, too. They prayed while raising their hands, kneeling, prostrating their bodies to the ground or standing. This kind of variety will keep our prayers fresh and expressive of the mood in our hearts at the time of prayer.

Staleness will automatically set in unless we deliberately effect change in our expression of prayer. Diversity of performance is one of the first things the Scriptures will teach us about prayer when we bring God's Word into our praying.

The Scriptures instruct us *while* we pray

Prayer naturally brings us to the Word, and God's Word will always bring us to prayer. The two of them go together like a hand in a glove.

Unfortunately, however, some people keep them separated at all times. They have their time to read the Bible and their time for prayer. Both disciplines are admirable, but they could very properly be mixed. During Bible reading, when something delights your spirit, express that emotion in a quick prayer of praise to God. If the Word seems to offer something you desire, pause in your reading and make that desire a prayer to God. Quick, unpremeditated expressions are a vital part of a prayer life.

I used to keep a small notebook handy to write down the things I was being inspired to pray for while reading the Bible. After a season, I discovered that the time I spent writing it down was more profitably spent expressing a prayer. The spontaneity is lost when we let time separate us from the urge. God loves the quick ejaculations of our spirits. Those natural cries of the human heart uttered in childlike sincerity are heard above the din of religious incantations that are called prayers.

The reverse of this equation is equally valuable. Not only can we extemporise prayer when reading the Scriptures, but when we are praying we can speak forth the Scriptures. The Holy Spirit often brings passages to our remembrance as we're praying. When we respond to those promptings, our praying grows to a new dimension. In our uttered prayers, we are expressing our wills to God, but in his Word he is expressing his will to us.

The Scriptures say this of godly Samuel: 'The Lord continued to appear at Shiloh, and there he revealed himself to Samuel through his word' (1 Samuel 3:21). Samuel learned to know God by the words God spoke to him. So can we, and the Bible is called 'the living and enduring word of God' (1 Peter 1:23). The Bible is a guide to God and instruction in proper prayer to him. Why not bring the Bible into your prayer life?

In the provision of God, there is an *interaction of our prayer and God's Word.*

The computer on which I am writing this book has a key labelled 'help'. At any moment, I can press it and immediately the screen fills with information that assists me to get the most out of the word processing system. All of this information is in the instruction manual, but it is far quicker to press the 'help' key and see the instructions flash in front of me in a split second.

The Bible is that 'help' key in time of prayer. When we get lost in prayer, the Scriptures help us find our way. When our praying becomes too introspective, the Scriptures redirect our attention to God. If we get bogged down in petitions, the Scriptures can redirect our thoughts away from our misery and towards God and his goodness.

As I am writing this chapter, I am ministering in a church that is in the midst of difficulties. A long-term pastor has been voted out of office, and the young replacement has made many changes in a short time. It takes neither experience nor spiritual discernment to be aware of the tension in the congregation. But God is breathing new life into the people.

Last night, following the sermon, I asked the congregation to gather at the front of the church for a season of prayer and praise. The honest prayers that followed reflected the people's hurts and disappointments, but it lacked faith and fervour.

I was pleasantly surprised when the pastor began to quote a passage of Scripture. I turned and watched as,with hands raised to heaven, he stood among his people and recited most of the eighth chapter of Romans. It was faith-producing. It directed attention to God. It electrified the congregation and gave them something to grasp hold of in their prayer response.

When the pastor finished, the people raised their voices to a new level of prayer, and we dismissed later on a note of victory. God's Word had prevailed. We had been lifted out of ourselves into the divine presence by introducing the Scriptures into our prayer time. Praying the Scriptures works!

One of the most frustrating aspects of prayer is finding the right vocabulary to express what is in your heart. Bringing the Scriptures into your prayer can greatly expand your vocabulary. I have found the

Psalms to be a spiritual thesaurus for my praise and worship vocabulary. The prayers of Paul expand my vocabulary of petition; the prayers of Jesus give a tailor-made vocabulary for relationship with the Father.

The Bible not only instructs us *to* pray, but it also teaches us *how* to pray and it does this *while* we pray. The more we know the Word, the greater resource the Holy Spirit has to draw upon in teaching us what to say and how to say it. This faithful teacher uses his own textbook – the Bible – and applies its principles, its provisions and even its expressions to our personal communication with God.

Good teaching requires good illustrations, and the Scriptures abundantly illustrate prayer. In its pages we see how praying men and women affected the course of lives and nations.

5

The Scriptures illustrate prayer

Perhaps the most popular books of the last decade have been how-to books. They cover everything from car repair to zither construction. Some of these books are practical and easy to understand. Others seem to be assembly instructions translated from a foreign language by someone with only a theoretical knowledge of English. The most useful of these books have been written by people who have mastered a subject through hands-on experience. These authors are able to give apt illustrations that help us grasp the subject.

This type of book is nothing new. The Bible is the greatest how-to book ever written. Although more than forty men were used in its writing, the Holy Spirit is the true author of God's Word, and he is an absolute master of the subject at hand. To help make spiritual principles understandable and applicable to everyday life, the Spirit gives us repeated pictures of men and women who are wrestling with the truth. This is especially obvious when it comes to prayer. Again and again, the Scriptures give us glimpses of people who grasped the tool of prayer and applied it successfully to problems they faced.

I can get discouraged trying to make mere theory work, but if I can see that theory demonstrated in another's experience, I take courage and try again. God's Word does not demand and fail to demonstrate. It not only gives an imperative; it gives an illustration. Often example follows example as the Spirit gives us step-by-step pictures of how to do what God has required us to do.

Since successful prayer is an acquired art, we need all the instruction and demonstration we can get. Anyone can dab paint on a canvas, but not everyone can produce a masterful painting. Similarly, anyone can offer a prayer, but not everyone can make prayer a masterpiece of communication.

We need a teacher in the art of praying, and the Holy Spirit is that teacher. He uses the Bible as his textbook, and he fills the text with how-to-do-it pictures. Under his tutelage, we learn that there are many different kinds of prayer. Perhaps illustrations of three types of prayer will help us grasp the importance of praying the Scriptures in order to know how to pray in different situations.

Scriptures illustrate prayers of *penitence*

When Israel's King Solomon dedicated the magnificent temple he had built for Jehovah, the Lord appeared to Solomon by night, and said to him: 'I have heard your prayer and have chosen this place for myself as a temple for sacrifices.... If my people, who are called by my name, will humble themselves and pray and seek my face and turn from their wicked ways, then will I hear from heaven and will forgive their sin and will heal their land' (2 Chronicles 7:12, 14).

This is a divine principle that works as well today as it did in Solomon's day. Repentance always opens us to God's blessing and presence. Few Christians lack this knowledge, yet most of us find praying an honest prayer of repentance most difficult. We excuse our behaviour with human rationalisation, and, even if we do admit guilt, we don't forsake the practice of iniquity.

Repentance is far more than admitting guilt or even feeling sorry for our behaviour. It will probably embody both of these, but true repentance is an 'about face'. It is a one-hundred-and-eighty-degree turn in behaviour. It starts in the lips, but it ends up in the life. It changes an attitude, but it also changes our actions.

The Bible gives us many illustrations of repentance, but probably none is more graphic than David's. After the prophet Nathan stirred David's righteous indignation with the parable of a rich man confiscating the poor man's pet lamb, Nathan pointed his finger at David and said, 'You are the man!' Then David admitted, 'I have sinned against the Lord' (2 Samuel 12:7, 13).

After the prophet extended God's forgiveness, David composed Psalm 51: 'Have mercy on me, O God, according to your unfailing love; according to your great compassion blot out my transgressions. Wash away all my iniquity and cleanse me from my sin' (v1-2).

When the Holy Spirit points a finger of conviction at us, we can feel trapped, exposed and humiliated. Our first desire is to run, but where can we go to escape God's presence? The cleverest response we can make is, 'I have sinned against the Lord.' That is the beginning prayer of a penitent person, but it should not be the entire prayer. That is only admission of guilt.

On occasion, when I have been unable to pray any further than this, I have turned to David's psalm of repentance and prayed it as my own. It continues: 'Cleanse me with hyssop, and I shall be clean; wash me, and I shall be whiter than snow. Let me hear joy and gladness; let the bones you have crushed rejoice.

Hide your face from my sins and blot out all my iniquity' (Psalm 51:7-9). It is a glorious model prayer of penitence.

This illustration of repentance shows us what to ask for once we have honestly admitted misconduct and asked for forgiveness. 'Create in me a pure heart, O God, and renew a steadfast spirit within me,' David continued (Psalm 51:10). We can pray that prayer as our very own. Only God can change our nature, but he will not do it unless we invite him to do so.

Some Christians repent and then live in a self-imposed exile from God's presence. They seem to think, 'If God isn't going to chasten me, I must punish myself.' It would be far better for them to join David's example of crying, 'Do not cast me from your presence or take your Holy Spirit from me. Restore to me the joy of your salvation and grant me a willing spirit' (Psalm 51:11-12).

Since we learn best by observing a qualified person doing a task, the easiest way to learn true repentance is by observing David as he pours out his penitence before the Lord. Then we should 'go and do likewise'.

The Scriptures illustrate prayers of *pardon*

There is a difference between praying *for* forgiveness and praying a prayer *of* forgiveness. We pray for forgiveness when we have sinned against God. We pray a prayer of forgiveness when someone has sinned against us. If we wish to pray effectively, we must learn to pardon, for in the model prayer Jesus told us to pray: 'Forgive us our debts, as we also have forgiven our debtors' (Matthew 6:12). This puts the measurement of our forgiveness in our hands: 'Lord, do for me *as* I do to others.'

Christ's further teachings on forgiveness were

pointed. In the context of prayer he said, 'If you forgive men when they sin against you, your heavenly Father will also forgive you. But if you do not forgive men their sins, your Father will not forgive your sins' (Matthew 6:14-15). Mark records: 'Whenever you stand praying, if you have anything against anyone, forgive him, that your Father in heaven may also forgive you your trespasses. But if you do not forgive, neither will your Father who is in heaven forgive your trespasses' (Mark 11:25-26 RAV).

It may be obvious that we must pardon others for deeds done against us and even forgive when we harbour bad feelings against others. But it is less obvious *when* this is to be done. Jesus settled this issue. He doesn't say we should pardon while in confrontation with the sinful person, but while praying to our heavenly Father. Forgiveness is extended to them through God. Like Moses, who earnestly asked God to forgive the sins of the children of Israel, we, too, ask God to forgive those who have sinned against us. 'Pray for those who ill-treat you,' Jesus said (Luke 6:28). Our prayer of forgiveness releases God to work in their lives.

The Bible commands us to forgive. Fortunately, the Scriptures also give us clear pictures of forgiveness being extended – even to those who did not ask for it and perhaps didn't even want it.

The model illustration is at Calvary. We see Jesus hanging on a cross after having been crowned with poisonous thorns in a mock ceremony in Herod's court. He has been mercilessly beaten under Pilate's orders. The soldiers who crucified Jesus had stripped him naked and gambled over his clothes. Looking at these men who had inflicted such suffering and shame upon him, Jesus prayed, 'Father, forgive them, for they do not know what they are doing' (Luke 23:34).

What a demonstration and usable pattern of forgiveness! We can incorporate it into our prayers when we feel the pain of injustice. We can and should cry it out to God when our slightest move renews the pain of any spikes in our hands and feet.

'But,' you say, 'that was the Son of God. I'm only a human. You can't expect me to have the same compassion as Jesus.'

Take a look at Stephen, a deacon who became the first martyr of the Christian church. For no greater crime than preaching in the name of Jesus, he was stoned to death by irate religious leaders. As the rocks bruised and broke his fragile body, Stephen 'fell on his knees and cried out, "Lord, do not hold this sin against them." When he had said this, he fell asleep' (Acts 7:60).

When the Spirit interrupts your prayers with a reminder that you are holding a grudge against another person, reach for one of these Scripture verses and pray it earnestly: 'Father, forgive them, for they do not know what they are doing.' 'Lord, do not hold this sin against them.'

It will free your spirit; it will release God to forgive you your sins and iniquities; it will grant God the liberty to deal with them according to his will rather than according to any desire for vengeance.

The Scriptures illustrate prayers of *petition*

Much as the pitch of a guitar string is determined by the tension between the tail-piece to which the string is attached and the tuning-peg on which it is wound, so truth is often found midway between two extremes.

In today's world, the humanist sees self as being in charge of life; the fatalist sees God inexorably in charge of everything. Each is an extreme position. The Bible teaches a balance between human participation and God's sovereignty. We have a responsibility to live uprightly in this world, but we also have the right and the responsibility to invite God's intervention into our affairs.

Jesus taught us, 'I will do whatever you ask in my name, so that the Son may bring glory to the Father. You may ask me for anything in my name, and I will do it' (John 14:13-14). He also said, 'I tell you the truth, my Father will give you whatever you ask in my name' (John 16:23).

Paul experienced the reality of this, and he wrote to the young Christians, 'Do not be anxious about anything, but in everything, by prayer and petition, with thanksgiving, present your requests to God,' and, 'My God will meet all your needs according to his glorious riches in Christ Jesus' (Philippians 4:6, 19).

The examples given in the Bible from Genesis to Revelation illustrate God's willingness to involve himself in our lives. God opened the Red Sea at the request of Moses, stopped the setting of the sun for Joshua and turned back the shadow on the sundial for Hezekiah. Lesser acts of God's answering prayer abound profusely on the pages of the Scriptures. God is concerned about us. He is not merely all-powerful; he has made himself available.

John summarised it beautifully when he wrote, 'God is greater than our hearts, and he knows everything. Dear friends, if our hearts do not condemn us, we have confidence before God and receive from him anything we ask, because we obey his commands and do what pleases him' (1 John 3:20-22).

This power of petition does not put the praying Christian in charge of God. Our prayers must always be according to the will of God. In the model prayer, we are taught to pray: 'Your will be done on earth as it is in heaven' (Matthew 6:10), and Jesus himself set this example in the Garden of Gethsemane when he prayed to the Father: 'Not as I will, but as you will,' and: 'May your will be done' (Matthew 26:39, 42).

The apostle John grasped this condition to answered prayer, for he wrote: 'This is the confidence we have in approaching God: that if we ask anything according to his will, he hears us. And if we know that he hears us – whatever we ask – we know that we have what we asked of him' (1 John 5:14-15).

Our prayers are less a means of persuading God to do what we want done than they are grants of permission that release the will of God in our world. Our praying will not violate the will of God, nor will it be profitable if it is outside God's will.

This makes knowing the will of God the major key to prevailing prayer. As we discover what God wants to do, it takes very little faith to pray an effective prayer. If you receive a letter from your bank saying that someone has anonymously deposited ten thousand pounds into your current account, it doesn't require great faith to write a cheque as payment for something you desire or need. Within the bounds of that amount of money, you are free to spend as you wish. The will of the donor was expressed in the no-strings deposit. You were granted a 'whatsoever you desire' within the boundaries of ten thousand pounds.

Discovering God's will and knowing the boundaries of his provision is not as difficult as we assume it to be. God has three major ways he reveals his will to us. An impulse in the soul, a voice in the spirit and the written Word of God all reveal God's desires for us.

God often unveils his will for us by creating within us a desire for what he wants to do. The Bible affirms, 'It is God who works in you to will and to act according to his good purpose' (Philippians 2:13). God loves to create in us desires for his will so that we will seek for the fulfilment of those desires. Often, when we are praying, we become alerted to strong feelings about certain things or people. If we pursue that in prayer, we may discover that God is revealing his will through an impulse to our souls.

A second way of knowing the will of God is through the voice of the indwelling Holy Spirit who speaks to our spirits. Paul told us, 'The Spirit intercedes for the saints in accordance with God's will' (Romans 8:27). When the Holy Spirit is in charge of our praying, we will automatically pray in the will of God, for he is the Spirit of God, and God cannot contradict himself.

The third way God reveals his will to us is in the Scriptures. This is the most normal and by far the safest way to know God's will. All inner impulses to the soul and spirit must bow to the written Word of God. For our protection God has guaranteed that his inward guidance will never violate his written Word.

The more we incorporate the Scriptures into our praying, the more likely we are to pray in the will of God, for God always stands behind what he has said. A classic example of this is Elijah. Having read in Deuteronomy that departure from Jehovah would cause God to seal up the heavens, whereas obedience to God brought assurance of abundant rain, Elijah believed God's Word and prayed about it.

James sums up the story effectively: 'Elijah was a man just like us. He prayed earnestly that it would not rain, and it did not rain on the land for three and a half years. Again he prayed, and the heavens gave rain, and the earth produced its crops' (James 5:17-18). What a powerful illustration of praying the Scriptures and getting God to intervene to do what he had declared he would do! Even Jesus referred to Elijah's prayer (see Luke 4:25).

What the Holy Spirit quickens us to see in the Scriptures is the will of God. We should pray it, proclaim it, practise it. It will put faith and fire into our prayers. As a matter of fact, it is often something seen or remembered in the Scriptures that initiates our praying in the first place.

6

Praying the Scriptures initiates our prayer

I am old enough to remember priming a hand-pump to get water from a well. I remember when the first aeroplane flew into Reno, Nevada, USA; Dad dismissed church early so we could go to the cow pasture and watch it. I'm from the 'old days', but I love modern conveniences. My computer has cut in half the time it takes me to write a book. I prefer my Thunderbird car to my father's Model A Ford.

But there is one modern convenience I am still very uncomfortable with: the telephone. I resent it and consider it a rude invasion of my privacy and an interruption to my work schedule. I consistently dislike having to use a phone. But, in today's world, I can't get along without it, so I seek to make peace with its presence on my desk. Fortunately, my wife, Eleanor, has an opposite view of this means of contacting the world from her kitchen.

When someone phones me, I am far more at ease than when I have to initiate the call. If I am in the office and can take calls as they come, my day progresses more smoothly than if I return to my desk to find a lot of call-back messages awaiting me.

To those who understand human personalities, I have revealed a great deal about myself in this confession. I simply have difficulty in initiating a conversation – especially when I can't see the person with whom I am speaking.

I have the same difficulty at the beginning of prayer time. Because it is difficult to 'place the call' to the King of kings, I often begin my prayer time either reading or, more likely, quoting a portion of God's Word. When it starts to speak to me, I realise that God has initiated the communication; he placed the call in his Word hundreds of years before I was born. The cry through the prophet is as valid today as it was when it was written: ' "Come now, let us reason together," says the Lord' (Isaiah 1:18). God is calling his people to talk things over with him.

The Scriptures initiate our concepts of God

When I receive a phone call, I immediately write that person's name on a piece of paper. Then I continue to look at the name throughout the phone conversation. Communication is far easier for me if I can form a mental image of the person to whom I am talking. Those who call and say, 'Can you guess who this is?' make it very difficult for me to communicate with them.

God doesn't play guessing games with his children. When he places a call to us, he tells us who he is. One of the main purposes of the Bible is to reveal God to us. He reveals himself to us in his names, in his actions, in his character and in his promises.

When he spoke to Moses at the burning bush, he identified himself as the 'I AM WHO I AM' (Exodus 3:14). Later, when Jehovah spoke to all Israel from the mountain, he introduced himself, saying: 'I am the Lord your God, who brought you out of Egypt' (Exodus 20:2). Consistently, through the Bible, God identified himself before he gave a message to people.

He still clearly identifies himself when he calls us:

That identification is stamped in the Bible. I have greatly benefited by praying the words of Jesus to John on the island of Patmos. Before sharing the messages to the seven churches of Asia, the Lord told John: 'Do not be afraid. I am the First and the Last. I am the Living One; I was dead, and behold I am alive for ever and ever! And I hold the keys of death and Hades' (Revelation 1:17-18).

This is a vivid description of the one who wants to communicate with us during times of prayer. He lives! Therefore, I am praying to an actual person rather than to a theological concept.

He assures me that I need not be afraid of him or of his contact with me in the prayer channel. This isn't a summons into court, but a personal call of friendship. He also assures me that this call is not interrupting some important work, for the work of Calvary is complete. Jesus is now seated on the throne at the right hand of the Father, waiting for his enemies to become his footstool (see Matthew 22:44). When God initiates prayer through his Word, he is calling us directly from the throne in heaven, and his call must be given absolute priority.

As difficult as it is to communicate with a person who has not identified himself, it is even more difficult to place a call to a total stranger. Paul faces this in his Roman letter: 'How...can they call on the one they have not believed in? And how can they believe in the one of whom they have not heard? And how can they hear without someone preaching to them? And how can they preach unless they are sent?' (Romans 10:14-15).

God isn't asking us to pray to the 'unknown God', as the men of Athens sought to do (see Acts 17:22-34). He has revealed himself to us so that communication with him can be relaxed, natural and meaningful. How often the psalmists began their poems with a reference to the nature of God! They were giving the singers an awareness of Jehovah before they entered into a melodious communication with him.

The next time your prayer session seems stilted and sterile, perhaps you might retrain your thoughts by reading aloud, 'Within your temple, O God, we meditate on your unfailing love. Like your name, O God, your praise reaches to the ends of the earth; your right hand is filled with righteousness' (Psalm 48:9-10).

It would move the prayer from the realm of the sales-pitch calls we get from the telephone 'boiler rooms' and bring it back to the realm of two friends communicating freely. Sometimes, after I have made contact with the Lord in prayer, I pull up a chair and invite him to sit and talk with me. It helps me shift my form of communication from a religious dissertation to a friendly conversation. There are times when I sit and read a portion of Scripture to him and then tell him how wonderful I think it is.

But, unfortunately, there are days when I get very formal with God and merely dictate letters to him instead of calling him in prayer. It's like some days at the office: I dictate letters when I could easily handle the situation more quickly with a phone call. Maybe I'm not certain the people are available when I want to talk to them, or maybe I am just too hesitant to initiate the call. But then sometimes my phone rings and, to my surprise, the person on the other end of the line is the very person to whom I am dictating a letter.

What a relief it is to transact the business through conversation rather than with a letter! Usually I gain some additional information from the person, and I always enjoy the fellowship the call affords.

Similarly, at about the time I'm dictating prayers to God, he often places a call to me by quickening my mind to remember a passage of Scripture through which he communicates to me. What a relief! We get the business transacted, and I enjoy a precious time of fellowship with Christ Jesus.

The Scriptures initiate our conversation with God

Sometimes I receive a phone call from a person who talks in such generalities that I can't determine the purpose for the call.

It goes something like this: 'Hello! How are you doing? Just thinking about you and thought I'd call. It's been a long time since we've seen each other....' This is apt to be a person I met at a convention, but with whom I have no close friendship. It is difficult for me to get into such a conversation.

God's call to prayer is not that general and impersonal. The same Scriptures that initiate the call also initiate the conversation. His knowledge of us is complete, and he has given us enough revelation of himself for us to be able to respond to him knowledgeably. Beyond this, God usually chooses the topic of conversation. After all, he did place the call, didn't he? If we mix the Scriptures with our prayers, we will find a proper topic to discuss with God.

Meaningful conversation is difficult when we are weighed down with care. When I arrive home from a protracted tour of ministry, I sometimes sense tension in my wife. At first our conversation together crackles with interference much like heavy static on the radio. Because she knows I am tired, she often insists that nothing is wrong. Eventually, however, she gets around to saying, 'I hate to unload on you when you've just got home, but...,' and then she pours out whatever frustration has overcome her in my absence. Once I have listened to her problem and have assured her that we'll work it out, meaningful conversation is restored between us.

I was not her problem. Often I was uninvolved in

her pressure, but, as her husband, I was the one who could help bring a solution to the problem.

That is the way it is when we begin to talk to God in prayer. We try to be brave and pretend that everything is all right, but there is a conversational block between us. Even when the Scriptures initiate the call to prayer, most of our prayers start with petitions of one sort or another. This is why the Scriptures say that prayer involves casting 'all your anxiety on him because he cares for you' (1 Peter 5:7).

When we unload our anxieties, we are able to respond mentally and emotionally to our time with the Lord. Asaph learned this, for God told him, 'Call upon me in the day of trouble; I will deliver you, and you will honour me' (Psalm 50:15).

One way we can initially get involved in a conversation is to say back to the person what he or she has said to us. When someone says, 'It's been a long time since I've seen you,' we often respond, 'Yes! It has been a long time.' When a person declares, 'I love you,' the normal response is, 'I love you, too.'

Praying the Scriptures helps us in this responsive kind of prayer. When we read in the Scriptures: 'The Lord your God in your midst, the Mighty One, will save; he will rejoice over you with gladness, he will quiet you in his love, he will rejoice over you with singing' (Zephaniah 3:17 RAV), we can use it as a prompting for us to pray, 'I rejoice in you, O Mighty God. I rest in your love, and I sing songs of gladness when in your presence.' We are paraphrasing back to God what he said to us in initiating the conversation. We can do this with many passages in God's Word. Whenever God speaks to us, we can respond in kind to him.

Response by paraphrase or repetition can get boring in a conversation if carried to an extreme. It is, however, a wonderful way to break the ice, to find a common ground of communication and to launch the conversation into a spontaneous two-way dialogue. Just as there is often a season of give-and-take in a phone conversation until something 'sparks' and the communication becomes meaningful, likewise, in prayer, we sometimes interact with the Scriptures until the warmth of the Spirit within us gives us a fresh subject to talk about.

We do well to go with this new inspiration until we have exhausted it; then we can come back to the Scriptures and interact with them until something is again energised in our souls.

In the service this evening, the congregational singing brought the people into a rejoicing prayer and praise. After a short season, it seemed to exhaust itself. A woman in the second row raised her voice and prayed, 'Lift up your heads, O you gates; be lifted up, you ancient doors, that the King of glory may come in. Who is this King of glory? The Lord strong and mighty, the Lord mighty in battle' (Psalm 24:7-8).

The congregation quickly identified with this scriptural prayer, and the people once again lifted their voices to the Lord. Originally it was the song that inspired the prayer, but subsequently the Scriptures initiated further conversation with God. The first appealed to the emotions, but the second appealed to the reason.

The Scriptures initiate the context of our prayer

Sometimes answering the phone turns out to be a delightful pleasure. The caller has a good report to give. After the shortest of greetings, a friend tells me of God's special blessings in recent services or of something he or she has just seen in the Word of God. A caller is full of joy and wonder, which becomes infectious. I'm not expected to comment; the friend simply wants to report to me. My responses are natural and almost preconditioned by the excitement I hear.

Prayer has its similar moments. The Holy Spirit prompts our memories to review a passage of the Scriptures; the message we receive is so glorious that our inner being explodes with excitement, wonder and praise. In such circumstances, our prayer may be short in length, but it will be sweet in substance. We will spend more time listening than talking, but conversation requires good listening.

Sometimes the Spirit quickens to our spirits such words as: 'I took you from the ends of the earth, from its farthest corners I called you. I said, "You are my servant;" I have chosen you and have not rejected you. So do not fear, for I am with you; do not be dismayed, for I am your God. I will strengthen you and help you; I will uphold you with my righteous right hand' (Isaiah 41:9-10).

A proper prayer response to that would be, 'Hallelujah! What would you like me to do in serving you?'

Perhaps, while reading the New Testament, this passage seems to leap off the pages: 'When the time had fully come, God sent his Son, born of a woman, born under law, to redeem those under law, that we might receive the full rights of sons. Because you are sons, God sent the Spirit of his Son into our hearts, the Spirit who calls out, "Abba, Father" ' (Galatians 4:4-6).

It almost seems sacrilegious, but the impulsive response is to cry, 'Daddy!' If we bypass the censorship of our trained intellect and allow our hearts to say what they feel, we will enter into a fresh new realm of prayer. The Scriptures say that the Holy Spirit initiated this cry, so we dare allow it to escape our lips. It lifts us into a family relationship, where our prayer becomes a child's talk to a loving Father. They have not only inspired prayer; they have gently positioned us in correct relation to the one to whom we are praying. This automatically gives the prayer an intimacy it lacked when it was being offered as a business transaction.

Praying is popularly viewed as requesting from God, and so it is. But when we bring the Scriptures into our prayer, praying often becomes responding to God. Our prayer is a reaction to what we have just heard God say.

In his Word, God has introduced himself to us. He has initiated the conversation and has even chosen the subject that will dominate the conversation. Under these conditions, prayer isn't a chore; it is a conversation between friends who know each other. Could anything inspire us to pray more than this use of the Scriptures?

7

Praying the Scriptures inspires our prayer

When I am on the road, I phone my wife at least daily when I am on the American continent and weekly when I am on another continent.

We both know that I don't like to place a phone call, but continued communication between us is essential for the health of our marriage. Often I dial the number more out of a sense of duty than desire, but when Eleanor answers the phone with a cheerful 'I knew it was you! It's so good to hear your voice,' all resistance dissolves. After we have shared some of the details of the activities of the day and before we hang up, she invariably says, 'Thank you so much for calling me.' Her obvious pleasure at hearing my voice and her expressed gratitude for my calling continually inspire me to call her again.

Consistently incorporating the Scriptures into the beginning of our prayer provides a similar inspiration. God awaits our prayer, as surely as Eleanor anticipates my phone call. The Scriptures tell us: 'The Lord will wait, that he may be gracious to you; and therefore he will be exalted, that he may have mercy on you. For the Lord is a God of justice. Blessed are all those who wait for him' (Isaiah 30:18 RAV).

When worship leaders exhort us to pray, they often tell us to 'wait on the Lord'. But in a very real way God is waiting on us to pray. His Word has pledged, 'If my people, who are called by my name, will humble themselves and pray and seek my face...then will I hear from heaven' (2 Chronicles 7:14). Much as Eleanor schedules her evening to be available to my phone call, so God is on alert in heaven waiting to hear the call of his loved ones. What an inspiration to see in the Scripture that God is waiting to hear from us!

God not only awaits our prayer, but he appreciates it. Speaking in the voice of wisdom, God declares, 'I love those who love me, and those who seek me find me' (Proverbs 8:17). God never feels that our prayer is an interruption to his day or an invasion of his privacy. He welcomes and enjoys our time of communication with him. This also inspires us to pray.

Furthermore, God enjoys our calls. At least weekly my wife phones our two daughters in Atlanta, Georgia. But when either daughter initiates a call to Eleanor, I see the room come alive with Eleanor's joy. No matter what time of the day or night, a call from our children is never out of order. The psalmist felt that God reacts similarly; he wrote, 'The Lord takes delight in his people' (Psalm 149:4). Another writer of songs quotes God as saying: 'Because he loves me...I will rescue him; I will protect him, for he acknowledges my name. He will call upon me, and I will answer him; I will be with him in trouble, I will deliver him and honour him. With long life will I satisfy him and show him my salvation' (Psalm 91:14-16).

The next time you dread praying, listen to some of the passages of Scripture that assure us that God awaits, appreciates and enjoys our prayers. It will give you a fresh shot of inspiration.

The Scriptures inspire us with divine petitions

Granted, prayer is often a petition from us to God. But we frequently overlook the many scriptural petitions from God to us. He pleads with us to pray.

'Seek the Lord while he may be found; call on him while he is near' (Isaiah 55:6). When I read this in prayer time, I can hear God pleading, 'Please seek me. I want you to come into my presence and talk with me.'

Similarly, Jesus gave many injunctions to pray, and they were more than suggestions. As the God-man, he was imploring us to avail ourselves of this marvellous opportunity to approach the Father. He was petitioning us *to* pray much as we petition him *in* prayer. It is almost mind-boggling to consider that God in heaven is petitioning saints on earth to pray to him, but that is what the Scriptures teach. How this motivates and inspires us to pray!

The apostle Paul wrote to the young church in Thessalonica and pleaded with them: 'Brothers, pray for us' (1 Thessalonians 5:25). He had founded this church, remained in apostolic relationship with them and told them, 'We always thank God for all of you, mentioning you in our prayers' (1 Thessalonians 1:2), and now this outstanding man of faith is petitioning them to pray on his behalf. I am certain this request inspired this church to pray for Paul with a great, new fervency.

Apparently the saints in Colosse were already prayer-partners of Paul, yet he wrote to them, 'Devote yourselves to prayer, being watchful and thankful. And pray for us, too, that God may open a door for our message, so that we may proclaim the mystery of Christ, for which I am in chains. Pray that I may proclaim it clearly, as I should' (Colossians 4:2-4). What an inspiration it must have been – to know that they could be a channel through which God could open a door of service for this apostle!

The author of the book of Hebrews also interceded with the believers to pray for him. 'Pray for us. We are sure that we have a clear conscience and desire to live honourably in every way' (Hebrews 13:18). Although these people have long ago been promoted to heaven, the principle is still valid: God's Word petitions us to pray for the leaders and workers who have been given to the body of Christ. Reading these scriptural petitions in our prayer time will inspire us to pray for our own pastors, teachers and spiritual leaders.

James expands this petition from praying for key spiritual leaders to 'pray for each other' (James 5:16). Every member of the family of God needs prayer intercession from time to time.

When Herod arrested Peter and condemned him to death, the early church went into prayer overdrive. In answer to their requests, God sent an angel to deliver Peter from prison the night before his execution. What if they had not been inspired to unite together in such earnest prayer?

When prayer gets boring, perhaps we need to let the Scriptures inspire us to pray for one another. Many Christians have been dragged into a spiritual or moral prison by the enemy of the church. Perhaps, in answer to earnest, united praying, God will release them and restore them to active service in the family of God.

Through his Word, God is pleading with the church to return to prayer. God's petition to us to pray should inspire us to get involved in it. We need an inspiration similar to David's: 'My heart says of you, "Seek his face!" Your face, Lord, I will seek' (Psalm 27:8). Maybe we need to pray out loud these requests made by God and see what they sound like to our ears. If we won't do what God petitions us to do, it will be difficult to have faith for God to do what we petition him to do.

The Scriptures inspire us with divine promises

The concept of praying for those in authority over us governmentally and spiritually can be frustrating; we often find it difficult to believe that the prayer of an individual believer can have much affect on them or their administrations.

We need to remember that it is not our prayer that influences them; it is God. Our prayer releases God to intervene in the affairs of our world. We grant him permission to do things here as he does them in heaven. 'Your will be done on earth as it is in heaven' (Matthew 6:10). Our praying liberates God to do just that.

While it would be wonderful to involve our entire nation in prayer, God assures us that the prayer of one person in right relationship with God is effective. James said, 'Confess your sins to each other and pray for each other so that you may be healed. The prayer of a righteous man is powerful and effective' (James 5:16).

He follows this statement by summarising the story of Elijah who, without a prayer chain, intercessors' group or national day of prayer, prayed and closed the heavens for three and a half years; then he prayed again, and rain returned. One person who prays in faith from the position of a righteous life can make a difference.

Prayer is not a lottery that we have one chance in a million of winning. Prayer is a response to a promise, and God pledges his nature that he will hear and answer our prayers. This is a glorious inspiration to pray.

Beyond the assurance that our prayers will make a difference, we have a Bible full of 'very great and precious promises, so that through them you may participate in the divine nature and escape the corruption in the world caused by evil desires' (2 Peter 1:4). Unquestionably, the best time to plead these promises that will make us more like Jesus is when we are talking to him in prayer. The promise isn't a formula that enables us to change ourselves; it is a pledge that God will change us as we allow him to intrude into our lives.

Because God has elected to restore our free moral agency – our right of choice – he doesn't enforce his will on us. He offers it to us and demonstrates its superiority, but he will not coerce us to do his will. He does, however, invite us to come into his presence and let his love gently motivate our wills to submit to the divine will. This more normally occurs during seasons of prayer than at any other time in our lives.

These 'very great and precious promises' cover the full spectrum of human experience. There are promises that deal with the body, the soul and the spirit. Some of them deal with us individually, and others are offered to a collective body of believers. The Holy Spirit can inspire a passage of Scripture that can fit any situation in which we find ourselves.

Yesterday I was conducting a prayer session with a group of ministers and their wives. When the fervency of prayer seemed to lag, I chose to walk among them and lay my hands on individuals as I prayed for them. Most of the time, I felt a quickening to quote a verse of Scripture as I prayed.

It was interesting to see how the Holy Spirit chose a different passage for each individual, and that verse inspired renewed fervour in that person's prayer. Perhaps he or she simply needed to look away from self to God, or maybe hearing a promise of God rekindled their faith. It was proof that 'faith comes from hearing the message, and the message is heard through the word of Christ' (Romans 10:17). Hope may be inspired by hearing a testimony, but it is hearing the Scriptures that produces faith.

Just as an earthly father inspires his child to action

with the promise of a reward, so our heavenly Father stimulates prayer in us with promises that far exceed our wildest expectations. God's promises are always fulfilled. When Solomon dedicated the temple that his father, David, had so wanted to build, he confessed that he was inspired to pray a dedicatory prayer because 'the Lord has kept the promise he made' (1 Kings 8:20). Promises fulfilled always inspire us to prayer more fervently and frequently.

The Scriptures inspire us with divine power

If indeed, 'Nothing succeeds like success,' then nothing will succeed more than prayer, for behind our praying are the living and powerful promises of the Bible.

David sang, 'This poor man called, and the Lord heard him; he saved him out of all his troubles.' And then he implored, 'Taste and see that the Lord is good; blessed is the man who takes refuge in him.... Those who seek the Lord lack no good thing' (Psalm 34:6, 8, 10). David saw prayer as powerful enough to produce results because it dealt with the Almighty God who was able to do anything.

The Holy Spirit is most persuasive in bringing us to prayer, and the commands of the Scriptures are completely authoritative. But there is something beyond this that inspires us to earnest praying. God's Word is *powerful*, because all the power of God's inherent nature stands behind it. God said it, and that settles it! There are no promises greater than God's ability to perform.

The Scripture assures us, 'The word of God is living and active. Sharper than any double-edged sword, it penetrates even to dividing soul and spirit, joints and marrow; it judges the thoughts and attitudes of the heart' (Hebrews 4:12).

It is likely that the first evidence of the power of

the Word will be in us. God's Word is living, so when we incorporate the Scriptures into our prayers, God's life works in us. I saw this happen just last night.

This week I have been ministering with my sister and a most competent staff to a group of ministers and their wives. The sessions extend from eight in the morning until ten at night. Last night, the conferees were exhausted by the time the final evening class convened. Just prior to my speaking, a music minister was asked to lead some worship songs from the piano. He played a few bars of a song to get our attention and then asked us to open our Bibles to Psalm 150 and stand. We all expected to be led in singing this psalm, but, instead, he had us read it in unison.

I confess that I was amazed at the results. As we read that psalm with feeling, we seemed to release fresh faith towards God, and divine energy flowed out to each of us. The power of God's Word overcame the physical exhaustion we had brought into the room and inspired us to worship the Lord. The singing that followed was electric, the response to the teaching was thrilling, and the season of prayer we had after the teaching was powerful. We had been made alive by the simple act of reading aloud a portion of Scripture during our devotional time.

The Old Testament declares it and the New Testament affirms that 'man does not live on bread alone but on every word that comes from the mouth of the Lord' (Deuteronomy 8:3; Luke 4:4). There is physical strength and energy available in God when we use the Scriptures in our praying. What an inspiration this should be to 'pray continually' (1 Thessalonians 5:17)!

Praying the Scriptures not only inspires our prayers; it illuminates those prayers. When the psalmist stated, 'The unfolding of your words gives light; it gives understanding to the simple' (Psalm 119:130), he understood that the Scriptures illuminate our every contact with God.

8

Praying the Scriptures illuminates our prayer

In the midst of his distress, Job cried out, 'How I long for the months gone by, for the days when God watched over me, when his lamp shone upon my head and by his light I walked through darkness!' (Job 29:2-3). It is likely that all of us have our seasons of darkness where we can't seem to find our way. This is especially true of our prayer lives.

There are seasons when our knees barely touch the ground and the presence of the Lord illuminates our souls. How we wish it would for ever remain this way! Unfortunately, however, there are also seasons when we pray with ourselves instead of to God. Spiritual unawareness, or darkness, surrounds us, and we can't pierce it.

We increase the intensity of our prayer, but to no avail. We even lengthen the time spent praying only to increase the sense of frustration. We can't seem to discern if the block is caused by satanic powers of darkness, abandonment by God or dullness of our own spirits. Such seasons become a threat to our spiritual security and a detriment to our prayer lives.

Following his temptation in the wilderness, Jesus came to Nazareth where he had spent his childhood. 'On the Sabbath day he went into the synagogue, as was his custom. And he stood up to read. The scroll of the prophet Isaiah was handed to him. Unrolling it, he found the place where it is written: "The Spirit of the Lord is on me, because he has anointed me to preach good news to the poor. He has sent me to proclaim freedom for the prisoners and recovery of sight for the blind, to release the oppressed, to proclaim the year of the Lord's favour" ' (Luke 4:16-19).

The prophets proclaimed, and Jesus confirmed, that he had been anointed to bring sight to the blind. The Gospels attest a very literal fulfilment of the prophecy. There are more recorded instances of Jesus' opening blind eyes than any other category of miracle he performed. We do well to remember, though, that God is more interested in spiritual blindness than he is with physical sightlessness. Jesus came to restore spiritual vision to his children.

After years of walking with Jesus, the apostle John wrote: 'In him was life, and that life was the light of men. The light shines in the darkness, but the darkness has not understood it' (John 1:4-5). He also testified, 'The darkness is passing and the true light is already shining' (1 John 2:8). Christ is spiritual light, and he came to illuminate the lives of his children. While he was here on earth, he testified, 'I am the light of the world. Whoever follows me will never walk in darkness, but will have the light of life' (John 8:12).

On another occasion, Jesus told his disciples, 'While I am in the world, I am the light of the world' (John 9:5). There can be no spiritual vision without the light of God's presence. When Jesus was preparing his disciples for his coming death, resurrection and ascension, he promised to send his Spirit to illuminate the pathway into his presence. He said, 'When the Counsellor comes, whom I will send to you from the Father, the Spirit of truth who goes out from the Father, he will testify about me' (John 15:26).

All that Jesus was, the Holy Spirit has become to

Christian believers. 'Praying in the dark' need not be the experience of a born-again believer, for Christ has come to illuminate our darkness with his presence through the ministry of the resident Holy Spirit.

Praying the Scriptures illuminates blind eyes

Something about an embarrassing circumstance indelibly imprints it in our memory circuits. When I was about eleven, I joined my brothers and sister and attended a vacation Bible school held in a neighbourhood church.

When the director discovered that I played the piano, she pressed me into accompanying the singing. All went quite well until they began practising for the 'commencement exercises'. The student body was made into a massed choir of children, and the director chose to have them sing *Open My Eyes that I May See*. It is written in the key of A flat, and I had not yet learned to play in that key. I dropped it to the key of G, but there were unfamiliar chord progressions in the song that I simply could not transpose. I nearly destroyed the rehearsal, and when I asked to be relieved from my responsibility at the piano, I was told to take the song home and practice it.

I practised all right, but I practised the same mistakes over and over again. I was so frustrated that I decided not to go to the closing exercise. When the time came I arrived late and sat in the back row. The children sang well without me, but the director spotted me and had me stand while she expressed deep appreciation to me for having been the pianist all week long. I couldn't handle the embarrassment, so I ran home.

That circumstance riveted that song into my conscience. The words didn't mean much to me at that time, but I have probably prayed them a thousand or more times since I have entered the ministry.

Open my eyes, that I may see
Glimpses of truth thou hast for me;
Place in my hands the wonderful key
That shall unclasp, and set me free.
Silently now I wait for thee,
Ready, my God, thy will to see;
Open my eyes, illumine me, Spirit divine![1]

I have come to know that unless God opens my eyes, I can't see into the things of the Spirit of God. My daily cry is, 'Open my eyes.' That needs to be the prayer of every person who is experiencing a dark season in his or her prayer life.

I have often been convicted by the words of the Lord spoken through the prophet Isaiah: 'Who is blind but my servant, and deaf like the messenger I send? Who is blind like the one committed to me, blind like the servant of the Lord? You have seen many things, but have paid no attention; your ears are open, but you hear nothing' (Isaiah 42:19-20).

How often I have felt like a blind person leading blind people. There are days when my spiritual sensitivity is high, and there are other days when those senses are extremely dull. Occasionally I think I have the vision of a seer. But much of the time I can't see the wood for the trees.

This becomes almost hopelessly evident during prayer time. When I don't know the will of God, how can I pray it, or even submit to it? So much of our praying comes out of blindness. If we could see as God sees, we would never ask for some of the things for which we so earnestly petition.

We ask from a selfish vision, while God responds from a selfless insight. We tend to attack troublesome people in our prayers, but God declares, 'Our struggle is not against against flesh and blood, but against the rulers, against the authorities, against the powers of this dark world and against the spiritual forces of evil in the heavenly realms' (Ephesians 6:12).

When we realise that we are praying blindly and have no spiritual perception, we need to turn to the Holy Spirit for help. Of him it is written: 'The Spirit helps in our weakness. We do not know what we ought to pray for, but the Spirit himself intercedes for us with groans that words cannot express. And he who searches our hearts knows the mind of the Spirit, because the Spirit intercedes for the saints in accordance with God's will' (Romans 8:26-27).

I wonder if the Spirit is as much interceding with God to hear our prayers as he is interceding with us offering his help in our praying? God doesn't need help listening, but we certainly need lots of help in our speaking.

The Spirit helps us pray in many ways. But one of his favourite ways of interceding in our prayer life is by quickening to our minds a portion of Scripture that is applicable to the present situation. We quickly learn what the psalmist knew: 'Your word is a lamp to my feet and a light for my path.... The unfolding of your words gives light; it gives understanding to the simple' (Psalm 119:105, 130).

Sometimes we don't know what the true problem is, and the Spirit will bring a portion of Scripture to our minds that is a revelation of the real need. At other times, we fail to realise that God has promised to do what we are begging him to do. When the Spirit opens that promise to us in the Word, we move from pleading the need to pleading the promises. How often I have seen prayer sessions changed from an atmosphere of defeatism to a triumphant shout by merely introducing the promises given to us in God's Word.

Nothing eliminates darkness but light. And the

more light that shines, the less darkness there is. The more we bring the Scriptures into our prayer time, the more light we will have to guide us in our praying.

Praying the Scriptures illuminates deceitful hearts

On one occasion, God spoke to his prophet: 'The heart is deceitful above all things and beyond cure. Who can understand it? I the Lord search the heart and examine the mind' (Jeremiah 17:9-10).

To some measure, we are all aware of the propensity of our hearts to deceive us, but this deception is most noticeable during prayer time. We all seek to be noble in our praying, and sometimes what our mouths say and what our hearts feel are miles apart.

Some years ago I was waxing eloquent (waxing elephants!) in my Sunday morning pastoral prayer. The 'amens' from the congregation spurred me on to greater heights of expression. 'I love you more than life itself,' I heard myself pray.

'You're a liar,' the Holy Spirit said within me. I was so shocked that I stopped praying. The voice was so real that I thought someone had called to me from the audience.

In my momentary pause, which seemed like an eternity, the Lord brought to my attention the passage from John that says, 'We love because he first loved us. If anyone says, "I love God," yet hates his brother, he is a liar. For anyone who does not love his brother, whom he has seen, cannot love God, whom he has not seen. And he has given us this command: Whoever loves God must also love his brother' (1 John 4:19-21).

At that time, I was nursing a deep hurt caused by a false story that had prevented me from obtaining a position I had been promised and that I had dearly desired. Months had gone by since the offence and I had sublimated my feelings to the point where I thought they were no longer a problem. When the Spirit quickened this passage of Scripture to me, I realised that my deceitful heart was hiding my true feelings from me. Deep down I hated this person for depriving me of what I deserved. God was not only revealing this to me; he was declaring me a liar when I professed to love him.

There was nothing to do but change my prayer. Like a truck on a downgrade, I shifted my gears and prayed, 'Lord, I can't love the person who has so despitefully used me, but will you love him through me?' My wife was the only person in the congregation who could have known what I was talking about, but I wasn't praying to the people now. I was talking to God, for he had spoken to me through his Word.

Many months later, this person came to the house and asked my forgiveness for his deed. He had disliked something I had said and determined to see that I was not accepted in the position. I could easily have charged him for libel, but, by this time, God had healed my heart, and I saw more misery in the man than I had ever experienced by his actions.

If the Scriptures had not been brought into my prayer time, I might well have gone on for years claiming a love for God that was unreal. Thank God that in the same passage where he tells us that our hearts are deceitful, he says, 'I the Lord search the heart and examine the mind.' God's Word will reveal what our minds conceal. This enables us to be pure in heart.

David knew something of the power of God's Word to unveil his heart, for he wrote: 'The law of the Lord is perfect, reviving the soul. The statutes of the Lord are trustworthy, making wise the simple. The precepts of the Lord are right, giving joy to the heart. The commands of the Lord are radiant, giving light to the eyes' (Psalm 19:7-8).

Prayer is never more apt to come out of an impure heart than when it bypasses the Scriptures.

Praying the Scriptures illuminates God's will

As long as I think of prayer as giving orders to God, prayer is an unbearable burden: It puts *me* in charge of the universe, or at least of my own world. Prayer becomes a relaxed visit with God when I understand that prayer is merely giving God permission to do what he has declared he wants to do. The better I understand his will, the easier it is to pray that will and to submit to it.

Paul yearned that believers know the will of God. He wrote: 'Since the day we heard about you, we have not stopped praying for you and asking God to fill you with the knowledge of his will through all spiritual wisdom and understanding. And we pray this in order that you may live a life worthy of the Lord and may please him in every way: bearing fruit in every good work, growing in the knowledge of God' (Colossians 1:9-10).

There is no greater source of the expressed will of God than the Scriptures. As we bring them into our prayer lives, we are far more likely to pray according to the will of God than when we merely pray out of our minds and emotions. I must confess that I have often felt strong emotion for things outside God's expressed will, and sometimes I have expressed that emotion in prayer. When the Scriptures revealed that my lusting and God's will were opposed one to the other, I either ceased praying or I prayed, 'Your will be done.'

I recently took part in an ordination service for two young couples who have matured in their ministries. Seven ministers laid hands on them to pray over them, and several received and spoke forceful words of prophecy. One of the ministers opened his Bible and read a portion of Scripture that the Spirit had quickened to his heart. It was as direct a word to their hearts as the prophecy had been, and it released them to respond in prayer in a most meaningful manner. All of us were encouraged by this passage, and our subsequent prayer took a decided turn as we better understood God's will for these couples.

Praying becomes meaningful when we allow the Scriptures to open our eyes, unveil our hearts and illuminate God's will. It ceases to be small talk and becomes smart talk. It moves from merely expressing feelings to expressing God's will and our submission to that will. When God's word to us is mingled with our word to God, we have a meaningful dialogue that genuinely communicates. This, in itself, is sufficient to increase our prayers.

NOTE

1. Composer: Charles H. Scott

9

Praying the Scriptures increases our prayer

One thing we eventually learn about relationships is that they must increase or they will decrease. Only a rare relationship can survive sameness.

In a good marriage, the relationship increases through maturity, depth, mutual understanding and enlarged communication. The shallowness of courtship must be replaced with the depth of commitment. The deep desire to say what we think the other party wants to hear must give way to honesty in communication if the relationship is going to grow.

It isn't by accident that all ten major Bible divisions liken our relationship with God to that of a husband and wife or a bride and bridegroom. God wants closeness, commitment and companionship with us much as we want this from our marriage partners.

If we have to work at enlarging our marriage relationship, it is equally true that we must strive to increase and enhance our relationship with God. Since prayer is our main means of communicating with God, it is imperative that we increase the effectiveness of our prayer life.

Whereas our own praying is often the point of release of our love for God, it is praying the Scriptures that becomes the point of reception of divine love. How the Spirit loves to remind us of verses that proclaim God's love for us! When we repeat these passages in our prayer, we not only receive love; we increase the flow of love from us to God and to fellow-believers.

Paul knew that our human, Christian relationships must also increase or grow: 'May the Lord make your love increase and overflow for each other and for everyone else, just as ours does for you' (1 Thessalonians 3:12). Since God is the source of love, our relationship with him must increase before we can display an increase of love for one another.

John tied this vertical and horizontal flow of love together when he wrote, 'Dear friends, let us love one another, for love comes from God. Everyone who loves has been born of God and knows God. Whoever does not love does not know God, because God is love.... Dear friends, since God so loved us, we also ought to love one another' (1 John 4:7-8, 11).

Paul must have felt that we never reach the ultimate relationship, for later he wrote, 'You do love all the brothers throughout Macedonia. Yet we urge you, brothers, to do so more and more' (1 Thessalonians 4:10). No matter how close our relationship with God may get, it can still become more intimate. Even though our praying reaches great heights, it can reach even higher. The scope of our praying may have expanded to fill time, but God would like to have it increase until it reaches into eternity.

This level of increase is totally impossible apart from bringing the Scriptures into our prayers. All prayer ministry needs the applied Word of God if it is to enlarge, expand or escalate.

There is no virtue in repeating prayer phrases just to fill time. As a matter of fact, Jesus deeply condemned that practice when he said, 'When you pray, do not keep on babbling like pagans, for they think they will be heard because of their many words'

(Matthew 6:7). Rather than continually repeating what we have just said, it is far wiser to repeat what God has said. Our need is far less an important item of conversation than is his provision. Echoing our petitions after we know God has heard us tends to diminish faith. But recapitulating God's promises will develop that faith.

When we have exhausted our thoughts, we do well to turn to God's thoughts as revealed in the Scriptures. God reminded us, 'My thoughts are not your thoughts, neither are your ways my ways,' declares the Lord. 'As the heavens are higher than the earth, so are my ways higher than your ways and my thoughts than your thoughts. As the rain and the snow come down from heaven, and do not return to it without watering the earth and making it bud and flourish, so that it yields seed for the sower and bread for the eater, so is my word that goes out from my mouth: It will not return to me empty, but will accomplish what I desire and achieve the purpose for which I sent it' (Isaiah 55:8-11).

God thinks bigger thoughts than we think, and he never says anything he is unprepared to follow through on. Praying his words will stretch our thinking and involve us in his actions. This makes prayer so pleasant and exciting that we joyfully extend it.

The religious heritage in which I was raised generally practised extemporaneous praying. I recall with some embarrassment the first home prayer meeting I conducted outside our religious culture. It was a gathering of people from many different denominations who hungered after God. I was invited to come and give some teaching, but on arrival I discerned that the regular leader was detained; I was quickly pressed to lead the whole service. All went well through the singing and teaching, but when I called the group to prayer, I was startled to see person after person open a Bible and read a portion of Scripture.

My first reaction was to inform them that the Bible study was over; it was now prayer time, but the Holy Spirit mercifully checked me. I merely sat and observed as the people interspersed the reading of Scripture with prayers from the heart. It didn't take long to realise that they were responding more to the Scriptures than to the prayers. Faith and courage seemed to rise with every praying of God's Word. I gradually realised that what God had to say was more important than anything any of us had to say. Had we depended totally on spontaneous prayer, we probably would not have filled half an hour, but when we also prayed the Scriptures, the prayer time was more than doubled.

I don't mean to suggest that we should substitute reading the Bible aloud for praying, but when what the Bible says becomes a prayer from our hearts – it doesn't matter whether it is quoted, read, sung or paraphrased – it becomes a powerful release of faith, and it automatically increases the time spent in prayer.

As I have already suggested, when prayer is a monologue, it gets tedious and boring, but when it is a dialogue, it is both a teaching and a blessing. Prayer time will always increase when we give God equal time to speak.

Praying the Scriptures increases the substance of our prayer

During the years when I served as a pastor, I consistently asked for prayer requests in the public services. The petitions were quite predictable. About sixty per cent would involve physical ailments ranging from minor inconveniences to major illnesses. Nearly twenty per cent would involve financial needs; ten per cent would concern unsaved loved ones, which left about ten per cent for miscellaneous requests.

From my congregation I usually heard the same requests repeated in service after service. The very sameness made praying both boring and faithless. We tried different pitches of our voices and various levels of volume, but nothing we did seemed to impress God. We did receive some answers to prayer, but one request for healing was simply followed by another similar petition.

When we introduced the use of the Scriptures in our praying, we extended the latitude of our prayers. We discovered that God was interested in things in heaven as well as things on earth. We also learned that our church was not the full extent of the kingdom of God and that sometimes God wanted to pray through us for others.

I'll never forget what a shock it was to my congregation when I asked for public prayer to be offered for the other churches in our city. Subconsciously we had locked ourselves into smallness. When God moved in other congregations as well as in ours, we realised that the Holy Spirit wanted to be released in our prayers to reach an area wider than our limited vision.

I can't help but wonder if Timothy was surprised at Paul's admonition, 'I urge...first of all, that requests, prayers, intercession and thanksgiving be made for everyone – for kings and all those in authority, that we may live peaceful and quiet lives in all godliness and holiness. This is good, and pleases God our Saviour, who wants all men to be saved and to come to a knowledge of the truth' (1 Timothy 2:1-4).

What an enlargement of the scope of prayer! Imagine actually praying for kings and politicians.

How easily we forget the poor, the distressed, the homeless and the imprisoned unless we let the Scriptures prod us into praying for them. We who enjoy such spiritual liberty can't know the plight of the millions of Christians who live in tremendous bondage, those who meet together under the threat of severe punishment. When we let the Word of Christ dwell in us richly, we will be drawn to pray for those whom we have never met and about whom we seldom think.

The substance of our prayer will never extend beyond the borders of our experience unless we invest some of our time in praying the Scriptures. While the Bible marvellously touches the needs of our lives, it was written for the whole world. 'God so loved the world that he gave . . .' (John 3:16).

When we pray the Scriptures, our prayers take on the depth of God's will, the breadth of the world and the height of divine wonder. The substance of our prayers goes beyond selfishness to selflessness, and as a result we have an increased vision, an enlarged capacity and an involvement with the larger family of God.

Praying the Scriptures increases the scope of our prayer

I was travelling with a pastor when he brought up the subject of prayer. 'I try never to bother God with little things,' he said. 'I save prayer time for the big things.'

He had hardly said it when he realised that he would never face anything that seemed big to God. We both laughed and admitted that we all tend to filter our prayers through our own abilities and only talk to God about those things that seem beyond our proficiency. No wonder our walk with God gets so strained. We aren't bringing God into our everyday world.

Paul admonished all believers, 'Do not be anxious

about anything, but in everything, by prayer and petition, with thanksgiving, present your requests to God' (Philippians 4:6). 'In *everything*....' How long it takes us to learn to tell Jesus everything! Nothing is too small to escape his interest. Nothing is so secret that he doesn't know it. He has offered to share our lives, and he desires to share every intricate detail with us. Prayer is an effective way to enlarge the life areas into which we invite Jesus.

The promised effect of telling Jesus everything is that 'the peace of God, which transcends all understanding, will guard your hearts and your minds in Christ Jesus' (Philippians 4:7). As we share our thoughts and desires with Jesus, he shares his provision and peace with us. If we didn't have this passage of Scripture, we wouldn't know that God is interested in the little things of life and that our greatest peace comes from sharing little details with him.

The substance of prayer covers the whole gamut of experience, from the moving of mountains to the threading of a needle. Prayer should be concerned with the conversion of a nation as well as the comforting of a child. Prayer affects the heavens, but it also alters the heart. Elijah prayed and closed the heavens from raining. The sinner prayed and cleansed his heart before God. The scope of prayer is so mind-boggling that it takes the illumination of the Scriptures to help us see its perimeters.

When we pray with our own understanding, we often pray far beneath the purposes of God. We talk to God as though he were as limited as we are. We petition as though he reached out to us in poverty rather than in plenty, and we hesitate to plead with him to do what seems beyond the bounds of natural reason.

Last year my wife's older sister was diagnosed as having incurable cancer. Doctors said her bones were deteriorating. The number of growths in her body precluded surgery. One growth was so large that it had broken some ribs. When the doctor gave her two months to live, her family travelled to be at her bedside. As Eleanor and I flew to the state of Washington, I tried to prepare her for the imminent death of her sister, Dorothy. She seemed ready to accept it, and after spending a few days at Dorothy's side, we were all convinced that the doctor had been optimistic. Dorothy already looked like death warmed up.

We prayed with her, read the Scriptures to her and parted for Arizona with the assurance that we would meet in heaven in the not-too-distant future. Once home, my wife phoned her sister daily to encourage her and pray with her.

One day, as Eleanor was praying, the Holy Spirit spoke the words of Psalm 103: 'Praise the Lord, O my soul; all my inmost being, praise his holy name. Praise the Lord, O my soul, and forget not all his benefits – who forgives all your sins and heals all your diseases' (Psalm 103:1-3). For weeks this passage of Scripture poured through my wife whenever she prayed for Dorothy.

To everyone's amazement, Dorothy began to get better. In the light of this, the doctor decided that some limited treatment would be in order, but he assured her that it would only give temporary relief.

'Who...heals all my diseases' continued to be the basis of Eleanor's prayer, and within a few weeks Dorothy was able to go back to her own home. She is now caring for herself, driving her car wherever she wants to go and attending church.

The prayer of our minds was, 'Lord, receive her spirit,' but the prayer of the Spirit, as revealed when Eleanor prayed the quickened Word of God, was, 'Who...heals all my diseases.'

How much better is the prayer of the Spirit than our prayer! Everyone in this family now believes in the power of praying the Scriptures, for they realise that God understands what he wants to do. When we let him pray through us by quickening his Word to our minds and hearts, we will receive what he wants to give rather than what we ask to receive.

Some people rarely pray, as they are unsure if their prayers accomplish anything. When we pray the Scriptures, we insure our prayers with heaven's underwriters.

10

Praying the Scriptures insures our prayer

It is difficult to deal with the unseen. The things of God are not unreal, but they are unnatural to our physical senses. We can't touch, taste, see or hear them in the same way we can experience a thunderstorm or enjoy a meal. Prayer requires the operation of faith. When that which appears to be fact fails to respond quickly to our faith, we tend to feel that the prayer has failed. How our hearts need constant assurance!

Just before reminding us that 'whatever we ask we receive from him', John declares, 'By this we know that we are of the truth, and shall assure our hearts before him' (1 John 3:22, 19 RAV). The Greek word John uses for 'assure' is *peitho*, which means 'to persuade'. We are challenged to persuade our hearts when we approach God in prayer.

This is easier said than done. So often, when we approach God, our hearts are troubled, fearful and spiritually cold. We pray, but we don't know if God is listening. We try to say the right phrases, but they don't even make it to the ceiling of our room. To make matters worse, the enemy takes advantage of our doubts and reinforces them with his words of discouragement as he discredits us to ourselves and insists that God isn't interested or even available.

John had learned from experience that 'if our hearts do not condemn us, we have confidence before God' (1 John 3:21). He must also have learned that, even though God assures us that 'there is now no condemnation for those who are in Christ Jesus, because through Christ Jesus the law of the Spirit of life set me free' (Romans 8:1), we Christians are quick to heap self-condemnation on ourselves.

Sometimes this is because we don't know the difference between the conviction of the Holy Spirit and the condemnation of God. Conviction deals with improper behaviour; condemnation is the sentencing of the Law. At other times, it is because we have failed to forgive in ourselves what God has completely forgiven.

Whatever the cause for self-condemnation, it will destroy our confidence during prayer time. That is why John assures us, 'Whenever our hearts condemn us...God is greater than our hearts, and he knows everything' (1 John 3:20).

My heart may be the Justice of the Peace, but God is the High Court. The ruling of a higher court always supersedes the ruling of a lower court. If God says, 'No condemnation,' nothing our hearts can say will overturn his ruling. God stands by his Word. When our feelings withstand the Word, our feelings are completely ignored by God. What a glorious assurance of acceptance this brings!

The blind songwriter addressed this when she wrote:

Blessed assurance, Jesus is mine!
O what a foretaste of glory divine!
Heir of salvation, purchase of God,
Born of his Spirit, washed in his blood.

Perfect submission, perfect delight,
Visions of rapture now burst on my sight,

Angels, descending, bring from above
Echoes of mercy, whispers of love.[1]

Our hearts may declare that we have no rights in the presence of God, but God declares, 'Whoever comes to me I will never drive away' (John 6:37). If God says, 'Come in!' who dares say, 'Stay out!'?

Praying the Scriptures gives us assurance

Nothing mechanical lasts for ever. Although I'm not greatly car conscious, I do need dependable transportation when I'm home.

Recently it seemed wise to trade my seven-year-old diesel car for something newer. I purchased a copy of *Car and Driver Buyer's Guide* and studied what was available. I settled on a model I felt would be pleasurable for me. Then I asked my brother Jim to do the legwork since I am on the road so much of the time. During the three weeks I was out on tour, he shopped around and made the best possible deal on my behalf.

When I returned home, he took me to the dealer, explaining en route that I wasn't bound to any commitment and could back out of the deal by simply refusing to sign the papers.

When I met the salesman, he immediately assured me that the terms he and Jim had agreed on were favourable to me. He gave me much positive information about the car, and, when I signed the papers, he introduced me to the sales manager who took me to my car and examined it with me for any defects, noting on the contract anything I saw wrong. Then I was introduced to the service manager, and he assured me that my service needs would always be cared for promptly.

I knew what they were doing. They didn't want to lose a sale at the last moment, so they were reinforcing everything that had been said and done in my absence. They wanted to assure me that everything was OK.

God graciously does the same for us. All his contractual arrangements have been made through his Son, Jesus. When we approach God to make this contract ours, he mercifully convinces us that all is well; he informs us positively about the product. He also gives us a pledge of continued involvement with us in our future dealings with him. He assures our hearts.

The inspired writer declared, 'Since we have confidence to enter the Most Holy Place by the blood of Jesus, by a new and living way opened for us through the curtain, that is, his body, and since we have a great priest over the house of God, let us draw near to God with a sincere heart in full assurance of faith, having our hearts sprinkled to cleanse us from a guilty conscience and having our bodies washed with pure water. Let us hold unswervingly to the hope we profess, for he who promised is faithful' (Hebrews 10:19-23).

What a passage to read when it seems difficult to enter into God's presence! We have a privilege of entry – 'confidence'. We have power to enter – 'the blood'. We have a point of entry – 'a new and living way'. And we have a person safeguarding our entry – 'a great priest over the house of God'. This enables us to 'draw near...in full assurance of faith'.

How can the devil withstand that assurance? What doubts in our hearts can long remain when we are praying this divine assurance?

Some time ago I knelt in the prayer room of our church, introspectively pointing out my failures to God. Others around me were rejoicing in God's goodness, but I was miserable with what I considered inadequacies in my life that week. My sister, Iverna Tompkins, walked over to me, laid her hands on my shoulders and most forcefully prayed that God would help me to get my eyes off myself and on to God's great provision for me. She prayed the words of James into my heart: 'Help him to count it all joy when he falls into various trials, knowing that the testing of faith produces patience' (see James 1:2-3 RAV).

'That's it,' my heart responded. 'It was only a test to produce patience, not failure.' The burning words of that passage of Scripture lifted me from discouragement with myself to delight in God, and I walked from the prayer room to the platform in life and victory. There was assurance in the Word that I could not find in my own heart.

Just as I was given a book of instructions and signed warranties when I purchased my new Ford, so God has given us written information that will positively reinforce our faith if we will but bring it into our time of prayer. Far too often, we lose heart while trying to do what God has promised to do for us. We should abandon our attempts to do the impossible and reread the Scriptures.

God indicates, 'I'm possible.' His assurance takes the responsibility off our shoulders and places it squarely on his shoulders. As long as we are doing what we have been told to do, we can be assured that he will do what he has promised to do.

Praying the Scriptures gives us reassurance

The Scriptures not only give us assurance that our prayers are *heard;* they also reassure us that our prayers are *heeded.*

John coupled these two assurances together when he wrote, 'This is the confidence we have in approaching God: that if we ask anything according to his will, he hears us. And if we know that he hears us – whatever we ask – we know that we have what we asked of him' (1 John 5:14-15). If we pray, he hears. If he hears, he heeds. What sublime reassurance!

We often act like the old gentleman who purchased a car from a used-car salesman who was gifted in accentuating the positives while eliminating the negatives. A week later, he drove the car back to the forecourt, looked up the salesman and said, 'I'd like to have you give me that sales pitch about the car I bought last week. It's beginning to act a lot like a worn-out car.'

Sometimes when the going gets rough, we need to be reassured that prayer isn't wasted effort. We need to be reminded that God on the throne is listening to his children on the earth; he is heeding everything they say to him. Perhaps we need to pray: 'Since we have a great high priest who has gone through the heavens, Jesus the Son of God, let us hold firmly to the faith we profess. For we do not have a high priest who is unable to sympathise with our weaknesses, but we have one who has been tempted in every way, just as we are – yet was without sin. Let us then approach the throne of grace with confidence, so that we may receive mercy and find grace to help us in our time of need' (Hebrews 4:14-16).

Praying this portion of Scripture will reassure us that we aren't merely granted the right to speak; we are guaranteed a listening audience at the throne of grace; we are reassured that the one listening has actually felt what we feel. It moves prayer from the concept of writing a letter we hope will be read to talking with a friend who has been through what we are going through.

The psalmist had reason to believe that God heard and heeded his prayer, for he wrote: 'Come and listen, all you who fear God; let me tell you what he has done for me. I cried out to him with my mouth; his praise was on my tongue. If I had cherished sin in my heart, the Lord would not have listened; but God has surely listened and heard my voice in prayer. Praise be to God, who has not rejected my prayer or withheld his love from me!' (Psalm 66:16-20).

When negative emotions seem to overwhelm times of prayer, we would do well to pray that prayer or the cry of another psalmist: 'I love the Lord, for he heard my voice; he heard my cry for mercy. Because he turned his ear to me, I will call on him as long as I live' (Psalm 116:1-2).

It is when we pray such portions of Scripture that our hearts are reassured, our faith is restructured and our hope is revived. No amount of praying our wants can accomplish this. We must pray God's promises if we want to be reassured of God's presence, his purposes and his power.

It is hearing what God has said – not God hearing what we have said – that revives our courage. The person who is strong in the Word will be strong in faith, and the person who couples that strength in the Word with his or her praying will be a courageous warrior in spiritual conflict.

Praying the Scriptures gives us insurance

When I purchased my new Ford, I was assured and reassured of the dependability of the car and the dealership through which I purchased it. Nevertheless, before I signed the final papers I asked to see the written warranty and a copy of the maintenance insurance I purchased. Past experience has taught me the wisdom of having all agreements in writing. To the credit of the dealership, I should add that all papers were ready to present to me before I even asked.

So it is with God. He has assured and reassured us of our right to pray and of his promised response to our praying, but, mercifully, he put it all in writing and signed it in his own blood at Calvary. It may be the shortest insurance contract ever written, and it lacks the legality we have come to expect in legal contracts, but it is backed by all the nature of God and the entire power of heaven.

It says simply, 'My Father will give you whatever you ask in my name. Until now you have not asked for anything in my name. Ask and you will receive, and your joy will be complete' (John 16:23-24).

Blind Bartimaeus discovered that this insurance policy pays off. When he heard that Jesus was passing his roadside begging station, Bartimaeus cried out, 'Jesus, Son of David, have mercy on me!' (Mark 10:47).

Although he was repeatedly warned to be quiet, he continued to make his plea heard. Finally, Jesus called him to his side and said, ' "What do you want me to do for you?" The blind man said, "Rabbi, I want to see." "Go," said Jesus, "your faith has healed you." Immediately he received his sight and followed Jesus along the road' (Mark 10:51-52).

Bartimaeus cashed in on an insurance policy.

The Scriptures give us the assurance that our prayers are answered. Therefore, prayer is not merely pleading our need. It is claiming the provision that heaven has offered us a written contract.

None of us would turn in a claim to an insurance adjuster without also offering proof that we have a current policy with that company. Should we not do similarly with God? When we merely pray our damages and desires, we are throwing ourselves upon the mercy of God, which is great. But when we pray the Scriptures, we hold God's written Word before our advocate in heaven, and this insures our right to adjustment.

Again, the model prayer given by Jesus to the disciples urges us to pray, 'Father...your will be done on earth as it is in heaven' (Matthew 6:9-10). God's will is expressed in his Word. We merely request that God keep covenant with us on earth as he keeps covenant with those in heaven. We didn't draw up the insurance policy; God did. It is his instrument of intent, and when we embrace it, all its provisions become applicable to our lives.

The more we understand about praying the Scriptures, the more we are aware that God's Word is the principal ingredient to praying. Without it, prayer is more of a gamble than a guarantee, but when we introduce the Scriptures into our praying, our prayers become more secure than the national treasury.

NOTE

1. Composer: Fanny J. Crosby

11

Praying the Scriptures becomes an ingredient of prayer

I bake the bread for our household. I have discovered that one can make many substitutes in the recipe, and certain ingredients can be left out without seriously affecting the flavour of the bread. But leaven is a key ingredient that cannot be omitted without disastrous results. Usually I use yeast as the leavening agent, but occasionally I use baking soda. On one occasion I used carbonated water.

I have discovered that as yeast is an important ingredient to bread and love is an important ingredient to marriage, the Scriptures become a *key* ingredient of prayer. You can make bread without leaven, but it will be flat and heavy. There are marriages without love, and they are strenuous relationships. In a similar manner, prayer without the Scriptures is both flat and painful.

The rest of this book will enlarge this truth, for we will see that praying the Scriptures gives imagery, identification, intonation, intensity, intimacy, incense, intercession and immortality to prayer. The one ingredient of praying the Scriptures adds more to our prayer time than anything else we might put into the formula. Its omission will almost guarantee failure in one's prayer.

The Scriptures give us the ingredient of vigour

There is absolutely no question about it. We are at a disadvantage when we seek to enter the spiritual world through prayer. You see, we are only one-third spirit, and we are communicating with God who is all-Spirit. When we seriously set ourselves to contact God in prayer, we almost immediately meet resistance from our bodies and our souls. Our flesh is uncomfortable in the spirit world, and our souls resist entering into the unknown realm of God's presence.

We need consistent discipline to overcome the negative inputs of our resisting flesh, but through the prayer channel we can enter into God's presence. Occasionally, God breaks through the barriers and approaches us here in our earthly realm. When this occurred in the Bible, people responded in fear and often manifested great physical weaknesses.

When Daniel held a government post under Cyrus, king of Persia, one of God's mighty angels communicated with Daniel, whose immediate reaction was to collapse on the ground speechless. The angel said, ' "Do not be afraid, O man highly esteemed.... Peace! Be strong now; be strong." When he spoke to me, I was strengthened and said, "Speak, my lord, since you have given me strength." So he said..."I will tell you what is written in the Book of Truth" ' (Daniel 10:19-21).

The sudden imposition of the divine realm upon godly Daniel was more than his flesh could handle. But when the heavenly messenger spoke strength to Daniel, he was able to stand, listen and comprehend. This strength came from the 'Book of Truth'.

The Scriptures are still our major source of spiritual strength, especially when we stand in the presence of great spiritual beings. When fear becomes overpowering and our flesh seems unable to function in the spiritual atmosphere of God's presence, we do well to pray the often repeated prayer of Psalm 119:154 RAV: 'Revive me according to your word,' or, as the King James Version translates it, 'Quicken me according to thy Word.' God's Word is a reviving agent. Jesus testified, 'The words I have spoken to you are spirit and they are life' (John 6:63).

John joyfully discovered this to be true. Banished to the prison island of Patmos, he was transported by vision into heaven and saw the Lord. He testified, 'When I saw him, I fell at his feet as though dead. Then he placed his right hand on me and said: "Do not be afraid. I am the First and the Last. I am the Living One; I was dead, and behold I am alive for ever and ever!" ' (Revelation 1:17-18).

The words that Jesus spoke became a source of strength and vigour for John, and those words are still a source of strength for believers. It is as true now as when it was written: 'The word of God is living and active. Sharper than any double-edged sword, it penetrates even to dividing soul and spirit, joints and marrow; it judges the thoughts and attitudes of the heart' (Hebrews 4:12).

We should never allow a season of exhaustion experienced during prayer to be an excuse to discontinue praying. We should pray the Scriptures to receive new strength. When our spiritual ears hear God's voice in the Scriptures, we not only lose our fear; we gain his strength as a replacement for our exhaustion.

Paul challenged the saints, 'Be strong in the Lord and in his mighty power. Put on the full armour of God so that you can take your stand against the devil's schemes' (Ephesians 6:10-11). He followed this injunction with a description of that armour, which pictures the Scriptures: belt of truth; breastplate of righteousness; shoes of the gospel of peace; shield of faith; helmet of salvation; sword of the word of God. Paul then ends by saying, 'Pray in the Spirit on all

occasions with all kinds of prayers and requests'
(Ephesians 6:18). It is during prayer time that we
clothe ourselves with the Scripture. This is our ability to 'be strong in the Lord'.

The Scriptures give us the ingredient of verification

Perhaps the greatest cause for paralysing fear as we
touch the spirit world is our uncertainty of whom we
have contacted.

When Saul of Tarsus was converted to Christianity
on the Damascus road, a light shone from heaven
and a voice spoke to this persecutor of the church.
Saul, later called Paul, immediately responded to the
speaker by calling him 'Lord'. However, 'The men
travelling with Saul stood there speechless; they
heard the sound but did not see anyone' (Acts 9:7).

Recognising the voice led to Saul's conversion, but
that same voice, unrecognised, served only to ter-
rorise his companions. Hearing God speak is not
what brings such peace to our hearts. The peace
comes in knowing that God is the one speaking.

In a far less threatening way, we often feel
apprehensive when a prophetic message is given in a
worship service. Sometimes the speaker prefaces the
message with, 'Yea, verily, this is the Lord thy God
speaking to you,' but sometimes we just aren't certain. We suspect that the message is coming directly
from the individual's spirit and not from the Holy
Spirit.

For safety, we must compare what is being said
with what God has already said in his Word, for God
will never contradict himself. Without this safe-
guard, responding to prophecy in a public service
can be dangerous.

When the Scriptures are introduced during worship this hesitancy disappears. God's Word is always
safe and sure. I've noticed that inspired reading of a

portion of the Bible often produces a greater response from the congregation than a prophetic word, for we can recognise the voice of God in the Scriptures.

This doesn't mean, of course, that we should rule out prophecy, for the Scriptures clearly warn, 'Do not treat prophecies with contempt' (1 Thessalonians 5:20). Prophecies should be judged, and the Scriptures are the basis for that judgment. Occasionally, when I have sensed a congregation questioning a word of prophecy that has been given, I have simply stated, 'This word is consistent with the Scripture,' and then I have read a corresponding passage. It put people's minds at rest and opened their hearts to receive a fresh word from God.

What is true publicly is equally true privately. As we're praying, the Holy Spirit within us quickens a message to our minds. We wonder if the word is from God or simply prompted by our imagination. In my experience, the Holy Spirit often brings to my mind a portion of Scripture that confirms what he has just spoken to my heart; this enables me to act upon what he has said.

Some may argue that Jesus said that his sheep would know his voice and follow him (see John 10:4, 27), but the Greek word used by Jesus for *sheep* literally means 'fully developed ewes'. The lambs don't know the shepherd's voice, as the discernment must be learned. They develop an ear for the shepherd's voice by observing what the mature sheep of the flock respond to.

Similarly, we Christians learn to recognise the voice of God. The greater our familiarity with the Scriptures, the better our chance of discerning God's voice from among other voices we may hear. As we bring the Scriptures into our prayer time, we learn God's voice; our fear of responding to God lessens.

The Scriptures not only verify the one who is

speaking to us; they verify our right of access to God. I do much of my writing on a small lap-top computer. When I get back to my office, I transfer what is in the portable computer into the larger PC on my desk. When I have linked the two machines together, the program immediately asks for a verification that this link actually exists. There is no sense in going any further in the program until I am certain that the two machines are properly united.

It is the same in prayer. We need to know that we have made connection with heaven, that we have accessed God, before we get too deeply involved in trying to communicate with him.

The Scriptures are our verification of that link. Paul, in speaking of God's eternal purpose in Christ Jesus, said, 'In him and through faith in him we may approach God with freedom and confidence' (Ephesians 3:12). And John, as we have already seen, wrote, 'This is the confidence we have in approaching God: that if we ask anything according to his will, he hears us. And if we know that he hears us – whatever we ask – we know that we have what we asked of him' (1 John 5:14-15).

When doubts grip the soul, praying the Scriptures will verify and renew our confidence and revitalise our faith. God has invited us into his presence. Sometimes it is valuable to repeat and thereby verify that invitation as we approach God in prayer.

The Scriptures give us the ingredient of vocabulary

Most of us are not really in touch with our emotions. Even those who are sensitive to their inner feelings seldom possess a vocabulary that adequately expresses them. Since prayer is the expression of affection, sentiment and even passion, we often find ourselves tongue-tied. The feeling is strong and valid, but the vocabulary to express it is unavailable to us. When we attempt to phrase our expressions in the everyday language of commerce, we fall far short of communicating what we want to say.

David must have experienced this, for he wrote: 'O Lord, open my lips, and my mouth will declare your praise' (Psalm 51:15).

Some people learn the language of emotion in poetry. Others learn it by trial and error. But the Scriptures are the greatest source of vocabulary that can release the deep feelings of the human soul. It is often said that every emotion the human spirit can experience is released in the book of Psalms. These writers were inspired by the Holy Spirit to put into words the thoughts, attitudes and feelings common to human experience. When we identify with these passages of Scripture, we gain not only an emotional release; we also access a vocabulary with which to articulate that release.

This principle is majestically evident in the events surrounding the birth of Christ. Very early in her pregnancy, Mary went to the priestly city of Hebron in Judah to tell her cousin Elizabeth the wonderful news. Mary hardly got into Elizabeth's house when the Holy Spirit moved upon Elizabeth, and in her greeting to Mary she quoted several Old Testament Scripture portions.

Reaching for words with which to respond, Mary, too, found herself unable to formulate into words her own thought pattern, and she began to quote the Bible. Her Magnificat contains more than seventeen direct quotations from the books of the Old Testament. She was using God's Word to give vocabulary to her deep praise.

Later, when Mary and Joseph took Jesus into the temple in Jerusalem for his dedication, the Holy Spirit told the prophet Simeon that this baby was the Christ of God. Taking the child into his arms, Simeon began to magnify God, and he, too, quoted a dozen or more verses from the existing Scriptures.

These selected individuals who were observers of God's great miracle of incarnation reached into the Scriptures to find phrases that expressed their passions. They quoted widely from passages outside the Psalter, showing us that 'all Scripture is God-breathed and is useful for teaching...in righteousness' (2 Timothy 3:16). We would do well to duplicate their actions by using the Scriptures as a vocabulary source to express ourselves to God.

When we are elated, how can we improve on the words of Moses, sung to the Lord after Israel had passed through the Red Sea and watched God drown their enemies in that same sea? The men sang while the women danced and played tambourines, 'I will sing to the Lord, for he is highly exalted.... The Lord is my strength and my song; he has become my salvation. He is my God, and I will praise him, my father's God, and I will exalt him.... Your right hand, O Lord, was majestic in power.... In the greatness of your majesty you threw down those who opposed you' (Exodus 15:1-2, 6-7).

When our hearts overflow with gratitude, the words of Hannah's great prayer of thanksgiving can give a fresh expression to our benediction. As soon as Hannah brought Samuel to the Lord in fulfilment of her vow, she prayed: 'My heart rejoices in the Lord; in the Lord my horn is lifted high. My mouth boasts over my enemies, for I delight in your deliverance. There is no-one holy like the Lord; there is no-one besides you; there is no Rock like our God' (1 Samuel 2:1-2).

Has anyone been able to express pathos as well as Job who, having recounted the great things he had done for others, wrote: 'Now they mock me, men younger than I, whose fathers I would have disdained to put with my sheep dogs.... Now their sons mock me in song; I have become a byword among them. They detest me and keep their distance; they do not hesitate to spit in my face' (Job 30:1, 9-10).

Many pastors have found themselves praying these words as a prayer to God.

Asaph found words to express his confusion over the apparent prosperity of the wicked in contrast to the poverty of the righteous. He admitted to God, 'Surely God is good to Israel, to those who are pure in heart. But as for me, my feet had almost slipped; I had nearly lost my foothold. For I envied the arrogant when I saw the prosperity of the wicked' (Psalm 73:1-3).

How often this psalm has given voice to inner attitudes that I feared to express out loud; it leads me to a proper conclusion as Asaph finally said the contrast was 'oppressive to me till I entered the sanctuary of God; then I understood their final destiny' (v16-17).

These, and many other passages of Scripture, offer us a variety of ways to express our inner feelings to God. By incorporating them into our prayers, we expand our vocabularies, extend the scope of our praying and express feelings that might otherwise remain buried.

Paul referred to languages of men and of angels when he wrote, 'If I speak in the tongues of men and of angels, but have not love, I am only a resounding gong or a clanging cymbal' (1 Corinthians 13:1). The Holy Spirit knows the language of *heaven*, and the Bible records much of this vocabulary. The Bible helps us release this vocabulary back to the courts of heaven.

The Holy Spirit also knows the language of *humankind*, and the scriptural record of human expression of pathos, exhilaration, joy, sorrow, hope, despair and all other emotions gives us a decided edge in releasing ourselves to God in prayer.

The Spirit also beautifully knows the language of *love*, and, in the biblical record that so tenderly expresses that love, we gain new insights into how to tell God that we receive his love and respond to it with our love for him. In our very expression of that love, our prayers reach higher levels of acceptance before the throne.

In my many years of ministry, I have heard more than my share of extemporaneous prayers. Some have been the expression of deep inner feelings. Others have been the shallow utterances of a person who put his or her mouth in gear before starting the engine of the mind. While God does not place great importance upon education, he is omniscient – he knows everything – so we should pray as intelligently as possible.

A paramount value of praying the Scriptures is to give intelligence to our prayers.

12

Praying the Scriptures gives intelligence to our prayer

God has never set educational standards for prayer. Illiterate people have prayed the presence of God into a community, while learned theologians have occasionally bored entire congregations as they 'prayed with themselves'. God sets no premium on education or ignorance. The requisite for coming into God's presence is to come 'in spirit and in truth' (John 4:24).

Still, prayer requires a measure of spiritual intelligence. Because we are dealing with a supernatural God, we must ascend to some level of supernatural wisdom to be able to find God, communicate effectively with him and enjoy his communication with us.

Paul prefers the word *spiritual* to the word *supernatural*, and I find it easy to agree with him, as nothing God does is supernatural to him. His work is always consistent with his nature. Everything he does is very natural to him. It only seems *super*-natural to us because it is beyond the realm of our natural understanding.

Paul, quoting the prophet Isaiah, wrote: 'No eye has seen, no ear has heard, no mind has conceived what God has prepared for those who love him.' Then Paul added, 'But God has revealed it to us by his Spirit. The Spirit searches all things, even the deep things of God' (1 Corinthians 2:9-10).

Since prayer enables us to enter into the unseen and deal with divine provisions that are beyond our natural understanding, we *must* have access to information that enables us to talk knowledgeably to God; we must be able to comprehend what he is saying to us. This requires divine revelation; the Holy Spirit is the source of that revelation, and the Scriptures become the channel for that revelation.

Powerful praying – praying that produces results – does require some spiritual intelligence, and the logical source of that discernment is God's Word. People without the benefit of a Bible have prayed prayers that God answered, but the great pray-ers of history have been people who were filled with the Word of God.

For our prayer to rise above the level of a magic rite or a religious ritual, we need some knowledge about the people involved in prayer communication. Effective prayer always involves a minimum of two people – the person praying and the person for whom prayer is offered. Usually, though, prayer involves even more parties – spiritual beings involved in answering our prayer and often people who attempt to hinder both the praying and the reception of answers to those prayers.

Without the help of the Scriptures, we remain totally ignorant about all these individuals.

The Scriptures give understanding of the person of God

In my recent book *David Worshipped a Living God*, I dealt with the nature of God as revealed in his compound names. In chapter two I pointed out: 'Old Testament characters were said to "live in their names", for those names so often unveiled the character of the person.... These names often reveal the fundamental nature of the person which gives us insight into the motivation behind their actions. Similarly, God has encapsulated his nature, his glory and his excellence into the meaning of his name. His name is one of his methods of causing us to understand him.'

Recently a new emphasis has been placed on praying the names of God, especially the covenant names of God, which cause us to understand better his nature in his relationship with us. I find it interesting that David, to whom the revelation of God was far beyond his time, declared, 'You have exalted above all things your name and your word' (Psalm 138:2).

I have meditated on this often and have preached on it occasionally, yet I have never grasped the depth of revelation contained in those few words. God declared, through David, that the Scriptures hold a higher priority in heaven than the names of God. God's Word is honoured even above his revealed nature. I am able to accept this as long as I remember two salient principles: God cannot speak in violation of his nature, and God gives priority to his Word for our safety. Even before I know his nature, I can know his written proclamation.

Moses, in the Old Testament, and Paul, in the New Testament, had dramatic encounters with God that brought them into a very personal relationship with the Almighty. If David ever experienced such a rendezvous, it isn't mentioned in the Bible. This, however, did not hinder David from coming to know God. He had enough of the Scriptures to give him an enlarged concept of the God he served.

If David could come to know God so well with only the first five or six books of the Bible available to him, how much greater our revelation should be with all sixty-six books available to us and in a great variety of translations! Perhaps we need to join the psalmist in praying, 'Give me understanding according to your word' (Psalm 119:169).

Many of us formulated our concept of God from Bible stories learned at home and in Sunday school. To that we added what we gleaned from sermons we heard. Sometimes the end result of this pattern is far beneath the divine biblical revelation. Since our intelligence about God is faulty, our prayers are equally faulty.

Job was a wise and a righteous man. When God allowed him to be tested, four of his friends, exceedingly wise in their generation, came to Job and sought to help him discover why this calamity had overtaken him. Neither Job nor his friends could answer the problem because their concept of God was far too incomplete. It was not until God came on the scene and revealed himself to Job and his friends that their responses changed, and God was able to heal Job and restore to him more than the enemy had taken from him.

We often wrestle unsuccessfully with problems because of an equally faulty concept of God. I have learned over the years that when I cannot get a grasp on the problem, I do well to renew my grasp on God.

This is illustrated in the story of the woman at Jacob's well. Jesus talked to her, but she responded with, 'Jews have no dealings with Samaritans.' Jesus answered, 'If you knew the gift of God and who it is that asks you for a drink, you would have asked him and he would have given you living water' (John 4:9-10).

She needed to see Jesus for who he really was and not merely as she thought him to be. As long as she saw him only as a Jew, her petition was basically, 'Leave me alone.' But when she saw him as the Messiah, her prayer was, 'Sir, give me this water so that I won't get thirsty' (John 4:15), and her life was transformed.

As we pray the Scriptures that deal with the nature of God we will also be transformed.

I remember one prayer meeting at which a wife requested prayer for her husband. She painted a rather sordid picture of him, and I gathered that she wanted us to pray that God would punish him. As the congregation prayed, the Spirit quickened the words of David through the lips of one of the people praying in concert with me. She cried out, 'The Lord is gracious and compassionate, slow to anger and rich in love. The Lord is good to all; he has compassion on all he has made' (Psalm 145:8-9).

Almost instantly the direction of our prayer changed. We pleaded for God's mercy and compassion for this man. He later became a key worker in the church and a blessing to many people both inside and outside the church. If we hadn't prayed the Scripture, we would have prayed the wife's frustration and anger instead of the nature of God, and the results would have been very different.

The Scriptures give understanding of the praying person

The prophet Jeremiah was told, 'The heart is deceitful above all things and beyond cure. Who can understand it? I the Lord search the heart and examine the mind' (Jeremiah 17:9-10). Long before this, Solomon had observed, 'The hearts of men...are full of evil and there is madness in their hearts while they live, and afterwards they join the dead' (Ecclesiastes 9:3).

While I realise that the work of redemption is to change a person's nature, I have lived long enough to recognise that the change usually comes gradually and far too slowly.

This is what I've noticed: When in a religious setting, we have a change of mind which deceives us into believing that we also have a change of heart. Much of our praying is ineffectual because it comes out of a heart that has not responded to the work of the cross.

How often our mouths pray selfless words even though our hearts are filled with selfish desires. It is easy to pray for God's glory to be revealed, when actually our hearts yearn to have our glory demonstrated.

Our human nature stands in great contrast to the divine nature. We are limited, while God is totally unlimited. We are usually selfish, but God is unselfish. We pray out of a nature that wants to get, but God wants to give. We want power and authority with God, when God wants friendship and association with us.

Our minds are great manipulators. We deceive ourselves into believing that we have become what God is and that we want what God wants. God, knowing the depth of this duplicity, can quicken to our spirits a portion of Scripture that gives us a look into ourselves. Though it can devastate our egos, Scripture, if we accept what it says about us, will greatly enhance our communication with God. Our entrance into his presence is never based on our goodness, anyway. It is based on his grace.

The Spirit doesn't leave us in this devastation long, for God's desire is not to build barriers that prevent us from coming into his presence. It is to build bridges that help us get to him. The same Scriptures that reveal the great distance between our nature and the divine nature also proclaim our position in the spirit world because of our relationship with Jesus Christ. The Scriptures say, 'You died, and your life is now hidden with Christ in God' (Colossians 3:3); 'Once you were alienated from God and were enemies in your minds because of your evil behaviour. But now he has reconciled you by

Christ's physical body through death to present you holy in his sight, without blemish and free from accusation' (Colossians 1:21-22).

Although salvation changes the way we feel about ourselves, only the Scriptures can reveal how God feels about us. How the Spirit likes to point out to us that we are sons, children of God, heirs of God, the family of God and even the bride of Christ! All these nouns speak of a high relationship with God the Father. When we pray from this position, we talk to God as a member of the family.

When we slip into self-condemnation during prayer, we need to pause in our petitions long enough to pray, 'You did not receive a spirit that makes you a slave again to fear, but you received the Spirit of sonship. And by him we cry, "Abba, Father." The Spirit himself testifies with our spirit that we are God's children. Now if we are children, then we are heirs – heirs of God and co-heirs with Christ' (Romans 8:15-17).

This revealed intelligence about our position in God will give fresh vigour to our praying and renew our authority in prayer.

Unless we pray with authority, we petition as beggars rather than communicate as sons. Satan will do everything in his power to keep praying Christians from discovering their authority in prayer, but the Holy Spirit will also do everything necessary to help us discover that authority.

When we pray the Scriptures, we discover the *authority of petition* that God has given to us. Again and again we are told, 'You may ask me for anything in my name, and I will do it' (John 14:14). We do not merely pray out of desire; we pray by directive. The prayer of a saint transcends asking; it is the expression of authority.

As we pray the Scriptures we embrace the *authority of declaration*, for we discover that we can have whatever we say. Jesus said, 'I tell you the truth, if anyone says to this mountain, "Go, throw yourself into the sea," and does not doubt in his heart but believes that what he says will happen, it will be done for him' (Mark 11:23). There are times when the Spirit so infiltrates our hearts with faith that we pray with the authority of proclamation rather than mere petition.

Praying the Scriptures also moves us into the *authority of restoration*. Just before his ascension, Jesus told his disciples, 'If you forgive anyone his sins, they are forgiven; if you do not forgive them, they are not forgiven' (John 20:23). While this passage has been the subject of many theological debates, it does seem to place an authority of restoration on the person who is praying according to the will of God. It doesn't, of course, make a saviour out of any person, but it does give us the governmental right, under God, to lift a person out of failure back into the favour of God.

We have authority with God, and we also have authority over demons and the powers of hell. How we need to be reminded of these authorities when we are in prayer! Praying the Scriptures will keep our proper authority before us constantly.

The Bible gives understanding of the ones who answer prayer

Prayer is not answered because we prayed; it is answered because the one to whom we prayed commissioned an answer. At the risk of being charged with polytheism, I suggest that there are four or more people involved in answered prayer.

The most obvious person is God the *Father*, who is the *provider*. Jesus consistently spoke of the Father as the source of all our need. Paul said, 'My God will meet all your needs according to his glorious riches in Christ Jesus' (Philippians 4:19). The more we pray the Scriptures, the more we know the Father.

The second most prominent person involved in answered prayer is *Jesus,* the *intercessor.* He intercedes on our behalf before the Father, and he intercedes on the Father's behalf for us. He wants us to know the Father as he knows him, and he represents us to the Father so that he can better understand us. He has repeatedly given us permission to approach the Father in his name.

The third conspicuous person who takes an active part in answering our prayers is the *Holy Spirit,* the *implementor* of the Father's will. Jesus said of the Spirit, 'He will not speak on his own; he will speak only what he hears, and he will tell you what is yet to come. He will bring glory to me by taking from what is mine and making it known to you' (John 16:13-14). The answers we hear, the illuminated Scripture portions that come to our minds and the guidance into God's will are all the work of the Holy Spirit implementing God's orders.

The least conspicuous beings involved in answered prayers are the *angels,* who are often the *activators* of answered prayer. Again and again the Bible shows angels as the agents of God who mobilise God's will. The Old Testament abounds with such incidents, and the New Testament begins with an angel appearing separately to Mary, Joseph, the shepherds and the wise men.

Later, it was an angel who released Peter from his shackles and led him out of prison. We know little about these messengers of God, but when we pray the Scriptures, their activity is often intense – and completely unseen.

What a reservoir of knowledge the Scriptures contain! When we pray those Scriptures, we are enlightened concerning God, ourselves and those people commissioned to intervene on our behalf.

Our praying makes more sense, and our understanding of God's answer to our prayer is enhanced as we bring the Scriptures into our praying.

Furthermore, praying the Scriptures helps to give us mental pictures in which we can identify and to which we will relate.

13

Praying the Scriptures gives imagery to our prayer

Paul was not only a great exponent of prayer; he was a man of prayer. Some of the great prayers of the Bible come from his pen. He crowns the magnificent prayer on behalf of the Ephesian church with the conclusion: 'To him who is able to do immeasurably more than all we ask or imagine, according to his power that is at work within us, to him be glory in the church and in Christ Jesus throughout all generations, for ever'and ever! Amen' (Ephesians 3:20-21).

In this great benediction, Paul contrasts the unlimited power of God to work on our behalf with the extremely limited people through whom God works. For years, I associated this 'power that works in us' with the power of the Holy Spirit, but I believe it is more consistent to the context to connect the power with the asking and thinking.

Isn't Paul saying that the prayer channel, made available to us by Jesus Christ and made operative through us by the Holy Spirit, is our access to this unlimited power of the Almighty God? Everything God is, possesses and can accomplish is available to us for the asking. This is like a personal computer on a desk-top taping through a modem the great store of information in a mainframe computer in Washington

DC. Everything contained in the mammoth machine is available to the PC – a screenful at a time.

Far better Greek scholars than I have pointed out that Paul actually piled powerful words on top of one another to make his point. It is comparable to heaping mountain upon mountain to try to demonstrate the height of God's ability. He assures us that God is able to do 'immeasurably more than all we ask'. That stacks four mountains to demonstrate God's proficiency to function beyond our wildest asking.

Then, in the original language of Greek, he repeats those four monumental statements and ties them to 'more than all we...imagine'. Our wildest imaginations cannot come close to God's ability to act.

Praying the Scriptures stirs our imagination

In Paul's Ephesian doxology, he clearly includes the use of the mind's imagination as a legitimate part of prayer. '[God] is able to do immeasurably more than all we...imagine.'

Obviously the mind is used in formulating the petitions we make known to God, but in adding *or imagine* after the word *ask*, Paul alludes to what may well be going on in the mind while the mouth is speaking. We seldom have the faith or courage to ask God for everything we are thinking. Sometimes we don't have words to give expression to those dreams. But they are neither condemned by God nor considered beyond his capability to respond.

The person devoid of imagination is very dull. Unimaginative people are usually boring companions. Major breakthroughs come through people who have released their creativity. Long ago I discovered that I prefer to read a book rather than see it portrayed on television; my imagination paints a broader picture than the screenplay can depict. Similarly, the person who refuses to allow the imagination to enter into his or her prayers greatly limits the praying. Our words may be exact, but our imaginations are often exotic.

The realm of the mind can be far more beautiful than the world of reality, and, if given the opportunity, it can often make some of that beauty tangible. We should bring that realm of existence with us when we approach God in prayer. After all, Jesus did tell us: 'Love the Lord your God with all your heart and with all your soul and with *all your mind*' (Matthew 22:37).

The logical part of the mind is not 'all your mind'. The imagination, properly sanctified, can greatly assist us in our prayer lives.

Right at the outset of this chapter, I want to handle two objections. First of all, I am not teaching imaging whereby we create a mental image of the thing desired and then produce it with the latent power of the soul. Prayer does not produce; it communicates with God who provides.

Second, I anticipate being reminded that Paul, in another letter, said that 'the weapons we fight with are not the weapons of the world. On the contrary, they have divine power to demolish strongholds. We demolish arguments and every pretension that sets itself up against the knowledge of God, and we take captive every thought to make it obedient to Christ' (2 Corinthians 10:4-5).

The old King James Version uses the word *imaginations* for *arguments*. Our spiritual weapons are used against everything, including our imaginations, 'that sets itself up against the knowledge of God'.

Not all imagination exalts itself against God. I have discovered that imagination, properly used, exalts God and leads us into his presence. Many years ago a woman minister who was a guest speaker for our congregation startled me by saying, 'Imagination is the first step of faith.' Only the fact that I knew her enough to trust her kept me from challenging ... statement. During her message she developed ... point logically enough for me to let it stand, but it had to sit in my spirit for a while before I realised just how valid it really was. Faith really does begin its operation in the imagination of the soul.

The faith chapter of the Bible begins with: 'Faith is being sure of what we hope for and certain of what we do not see' (Hebrews 11:1). Faith enables us to realise that for which we have hoped. It gives evidence to, or confidence in, things not seen. If our imagination has not given us an unseen something in which to hope, our faith can't bring it into being.

When Paul loosely quoted Isaiah as having said, 'No eye has seen, no ear has heard, no mind has conceived what God has prepared for those who love him,' he added, 'but God has revealed it to us by his Spirit' (1 Corinthians 2:9-10). The Spirit's revelation is inward. Since it is beyond our sensory experiences, it must be fed into the imagination of our minds.

When we divorce our imagination from our praying, we effectively short-circuit the revelation of God's Spirit in our prayers. This forces us to pray only what we already fully comprehend, and our praying never reaches into the unknown realms of God's disclosure. We so often fear that 'this is just me' that we quench the working of the Holy Spirit. He is limited to our faculties, so he must give impressions to our minds.

Praying the Scriptures solicits our identification

When read as ancient history, the Bible can induce sleep faster than counting sheep. We need to remind ourselves that God calls his Book the 'living word' and that it is as applicable to our generation as it was when it was written.

We need to read ourselves into the Bible. Sometimes simply putting our names in place of the personal pronouns can quickly bring the passage on to our experience level.

At other times we need to visualise ourselves as being participants in what is going on. In a conference some time ago, I spoke of Jesus' taking the little children on his lap. I used my imagination to paint a word picture of how he stroked their hair, hugged them and talked comfortingly to them.

Then I reminded the listeners that we are children of God. I challenged them to close their eyes and picture themselves approaching Jesus as he was seated on a hillside. I asked them to visualise his holding out his arms in invitation and then hugging them to himself.

At first, I was met with embarrassed giggles, but slowly the audience experimented along with me. Before long, I heard people say, 'I love you, too,' 'What a soft beard you have,' and 'May I sit on your lap?' They were talking intimately with Jesus. I saw tears stream down faces, and some used their arms to embrace the invisible Christ. What had begun as imagination moved into the realm of reality.

I received an amazing volume of mail telling me of healings that took place in the hearts of those who participated. Even today, years later, I have people come to me in conferences to remind me of the incident, and they tell me that it was a high point in their relationship with Jesus. My only regret is that many of them did not continue using their imaginations to bring themselves into the presence of God. They have memories of what was, but they fear to use their imaginations to bring them into what could be.

One of the keys to victorious Christian living is identifying with the Scriptures. Our salvation is an act of identification. We can't save ourselves. It is wholly an act of God in which we participate by identification. All subsequent victory comes by further identifying ourselves with the finished work of Jesus Christ. The natural channel for this is the prayer channel.

In my study one day, a person poured out a story of pain and grief and concluded with, 'Because of what I've done, I've fallen into the hands of God.'

'You couldn't be in a better place,' I said. 'You've been there all the time.'

Turning to Isaiah 49:16, I read, 'See, I have engraved you on the palms of my hands; your walls are ever before me.' I asked him to close his eyes and visualise his name written on the palm of Jesus' hand. 'What else do you see?' I asked.

Pausing for a long time, he finally said, 'I see nail prints.'

'Then every time Jesus looks at your name, he also sees the price he paid to redeem you. Why don't you thank him for such a demonstration of his love for you?'

That simple act of his imagination, coupled with the clear statement of Scripture, enabled him to identify with the Scripture and include himself in the picture of God's love. It lifted him from depression to a glorious expression of praise.

The Bible is full of life-giving promises, but they bring life only to those who identify with those promises. The ultimate end of such identification is the release of faith, but the beginning of the process rests in our imagination. Sometimes that resourcefulness needs a little nudge.

Kneeling at the altar at a conference meeting, I was sobbing my heart out to God. I had been profoundly moved by the ministry of Bob Mumford, and my heart was crying out for a greater depth of relationship with God. I felt a hand rest gently on my head, and I heard Brother Mumford pray, 'Father, "If a son asks for bread from any father among you, will he give him a stone? Or if he asks for a fish, will he give him a serpent instead of a fish?'' [Luke 11:11 RAV]. This is your son. Give him that for which he prays.'

This parable of Jesus was used by the Spirit to convince me that the heavenly Father wanted to give me even more than I was able to ask. I mentally stepped into this story and began to deal with God instead of my great longings. I simply needed a little nudge to identify with the Word of God.

Praying the Scriptures summons interaction

Until we learn to identify with what is being said in the Scriptures, we will remain passive in all our Bible reading. We'll treat God's Word as we often treat the preacher's Sunday sermon – something to be heard but not heeded.

If, in the passage before us, God declares his love for us, we should proclaim our love back to him. When we read a clear command, we should give a vocal response to it.

David was good at this. He wrote: 'When you said, "Seek my face," my heart said to you, "Your face, Lord, I will seek" ' (Psalm 27:8 RAV). David read himself right into the Word of the Lord. We need to do the same. We have long been reminded that if we meet the conditions, we may have the promises. Much of what God said to others is applicable to us if we will identify with the promise and include ourselves in it.

The parables of Jesus are of little value unless we can place ourselves in the stories as a participant. The backslider who interacts with the story of the prodigal son soon finds himself back in fellowship with the Father. That is why Jesus told such stories. He wanted to hook us and draw us into the necessary action to produce change.

Often, when teaching praise to a congregation, I

divide the audience into two groups. I remind them of the assembly of Israel in the valley between the mountains of Ebal and Gerizim while the priesthood was divided into two companies on these mountains. The priests on Mount Gerizim read the blessings of the law, to which the people responded, 'Amen, amen.' The priests on Mount Ebal read the cursings of the law to which the people gave the same response (see Deuteronomy 11:29).

Then I invite them to turn to Psalm 136 – the psalm that ends every verse with: 'His love endures for ever.' I have one group read the first part of a verse, while the other group responds, 'His love endures for ever.' Midway through the psalm, I change the assignment.

Without exception, this simple interplay with the Scripture has brought a wave of rejoicing and praise from the people. They had heard the psalm repeatedly, but actually calling it out one to another made them participants, and they had a fresh interaction with the Scriptures.

Far too often, we fear innovation in prayer time, but sameness is more apt to kill a prayer meeting than is innovation. Knowing that by praying the Scriptures we pray with a double anointing, we should not hesitate to bring the Scriptures into our prayers in new ways. The goal is never novelty; it is interaction, but sometimes a novel approach will encourage fresh involvement with God in his Word.

We should unbridle our imaginations when we pray. As we pray the Scriptures, we need to identify clearly with what God is saying to us, and then we can interact obediently with what God has said. This brings prayer into a two-way communication that is meaningful.

When we can identify with the Scriptures in prayer, it is an easy step to allow the Scriptures to give identification to our prayer.

14

Praying the Scriptures gives identification to our prayer

The first step in prayer is usually the most difficult. We can bring our bodies to the place of worship, and we may even compel our minds to focus on spiritual things, but getting our spirits to rise up and reach out to God is often a challenge beyond our abilities. All too frequently we settle for participating in or identifying with a religious ritual rather than stirring up our spirits to action.

Nehemiah and Ezra must have understood this problem. Ezra had led hundreds of Israelites out of their captivity in Babylon to resettle in the Holy Land and to rebuild the temple. Nehemiah followed some years later and supervised the reconstruction of the walls and the re-establishing of government in the land.

Once the gates were hung, these two men united to bring the people together in the open square in front of the Water Gate. The temple was now erected; the walls were reconstructed; it was time to restore worship.

When the people were assembled, 'Ezra the scribe stood on a high wooden platform built for the occasion.... Ezra opened the book. All the people could see him because he was standing above them; and as he opened it, all the people stood up. Ezra praised the Lord, the great God; and all the people lifted their hands and responded, "Amen! Amen!" Then they bowed down and worshipped the Lord with their faces to the ground' (Nehemiah 8:4-6).

Ezra wisely opened the gathering with the Word of God which led the people to worship the God of the Word. It is not by accident that the liturgical churches begin their services with a 'call to worship', which is often a portion of Scripture. This is what Ezra did. He broke up the conversations and directed their souls and spirits to God by reading a portion of the Law of God.

Just as conversation is easier if someone else initiates it, prayer is simpler if God inaugurates it. Beginning our worship season with a portion of the Word, whether it is read, quoted or sung, often helps our spirits identify with the Spirit of God. Once that contact is firm, worship can flow.

Even in our private devotions, we do ourselves a favour by introducing the Scriptures into our prayers very early in the process. It will give strength to the spirit, direction to the mind, motivation to the soul and, quite often, opportunity for the body to express action.

Praying the Scriptures can get every part of us involved with God, and that is the heart of true worship as defined by Jesus: 'Love the Lord your God with all your heart and with all your soul and with all your mind and with all your strength' (Mark 12:30). Praying the Scriptures tends to focus the entire being of the praying person.

Praying the Scriptures helps us to perceive prayer

As much as we would like to believe that all of us instantly recognise prayer, it just isn't true.

I have incorporated prayer in my sermons and, because I had my eyes open and didn't use the standard format for praying, few people present recognised when I shifted from talking to them and began talking to God. Sometimes I have heard people single out that portion of the sermon as the most powerful, and yet they didn't realise that it really was not a part of the sermon, but a brief communication to God.

Conversely, at times the person trying to pray doesn't get close to true prayer. Jesus taught this in a simple parable:

'Two men went up to the temple to pray, one a Pharisee and the other a tax collector. The Pharisee stood up and prayed *about himself*, 'God, I thank you that I am not like other men – robbers, evildoers, adulterers – or even like this tax collector. I fast twice a week and give a tenth of all I get.'

'But the tax collector stood at a distance. He would not even look up to heaven, but beat his breast and said, 'God, have mercy on me, a sinner.'

'I tell you that this man, rather than the other, went home justified before God. For everyone who exalts himself will be humbled, and he who humbles himself will be exalted' (Luke 18:10-14).

This type of praying is especially evident in public prayers. Somehow we feel that we need to remind God of our goodness, of others' sins; we give him all the latest news of the world. At other times we use the public prayer as a forum to moralise and pontificate to our listeners. In the religious use of the word, this is prayer, but it falls far short of the Bible's definition. True prayer is communicating with God, not with people about God.

When the disciples asked Jesus to teach them to pray, he gave them a model prayer to follow. That prayer has primed many people into a prayer procedure, but it is not the only scriptural model of prayer. The letters of Paul abound with brief prayers he prayed on behalf of the believers. Reading them aloud will not only instruct us in methods of prayer; it will inspire prayer and often become the vocabulary of our own cries to God. His brief prayer in the beginning of his letter to the church in Philippi could wisely be incorporated in our prayers one for another:

'This is my prayer: that your love may abound more and more in knowledge and depth of insight, so that you may be able to discern what is best and may be pure and blameless until the day of Christ, filled with the fruit of righteousness that comes through Jesus Christ – to the glory and praise of God' (Philippians 1:9-11).

There are times when we don't actually know if we are praying or not. We confuse worry with prayer and equate meditation with supplication. It isn't prayer until our desire becomes a petition. One of the sons of Korah wrote: 'O Lord, the God who saves me, day and night I cry out before you. May my prayer come before you; turn your ear to my cry.... I call to you, O Lord, every day; I spread out my hands to you.... I cry to you for help, O Lord; in the morning my prayer comes before you' (Psalm 88:1-2, 9, 13).

The context of his prayer demonstrates much anxiety, but he says that it is the asking that is the prayer, not the anxiety.

Another psalmist spoke similarly about prayer. He wrote: 'I love the Lord, for he heard my voice; he heard my cry for mercy. Because he turned his ear to me, I will call on him as long as I live' (Psalm 116:1-2).

David held a similar view of prayer. When he was in the cave, he wrote, 'I cry aloud to the Lord; I lift up my voice to the Lord for mercy. I pour out my complaint before him; before him I tell my trouble' (Psalm 142:1-2).

These praying men had learned to perceive the difference between apprehension and supplication. When we bring the Scriptures into our praying, we, too, will recognise the distinction between communion with our own heart and communion with God.

Praying the Scriptures helps us to classify prayer

All prayer is not created equal. There are different kinds of prayer, dissimilar motivations for prayer and unique ways of presenting prayer. There are also ascending levels of prayer. In an earlier book, *The Secret of Personal Prayer*, I wrote:

'Just as no one food will consistently meet the needs of the human body, so no one form of prayer will constantly meet the needs of the soul-spirit within us. God has provided ascending levels of communication that meet higher and higher needs in our lives. These levels bring us into greater degrees of the presence of God and give us fuller revelations of his nature. No one level of prayer can bring us into a complete fellowship with God. In any prayer session, we may move through eight or nine different levels of prayer, always ascending higher and higher into the revelation of God.'

In that book I listed nine different kinds or levels of prayer that are common to Christians: confession, petition, communication, intercession, the release of faith, submission, thanksgiving, praise and adoration. All are valid and each has a season when it is vital to the believer.

Unless we bring the Scriptures into our praying, we run the risk of locking into one or two forms of prayer without actually realising that other patterns are available to us. This will limit our expressions to God and likely bring a staleness in our spirits.

The Holy Spirit, who assists us in our praying, is a person. As such, he has all the moods of personality. Sometimes he prays a rejoicing prayer; at other times he cries out a prayer of repentance. He may move from laughter to tears in his intercession through us, but it is all anointed prayer.

At times our personal moods swing the pendulum of prayer from one extreme to another, and none is rejected by the Lord. All of them can find Scripture portions that will give expression in a God-pleasing manner. How often I have joined David in his prayers of frustration, then find myself moving into his cries of trust and triumph. By praying with his prayer, I came into a victory similar to his. Without the help of the Scriptures, I might well have prayed myself into deeper and deeper frustration.

Some of the prayers of Scripture are passive. The praying person seems so submissive to God's will that he or she hardly expresses a personal will. These are not easy prayers for Westerners to pray, but there is a time when they need to be prayed. When we view the sovereignty of God and see his purposes at work, our prayer can become very complacent; we are available if needed, but we recognise that he is in charge of the operation.

In other biblical accounts the person is extremely persistent in prayer. Elijah on Mount Carmel is an outstanding example. Having prayed down fire from heaven to consume the sacrifice, he again climbed the mountain to pray for rain. Six times his servant returned from his observation point to announce that there was no sign of rain. Elijah kept praying. Then the seventh time he reported that a small cloud appeared on the horizon. From this beginning, an immense deluge of rain fell on the parched earth. Elijah just wouldn't give up until God answered.

At times we need this tenacity in prayer. If we have a promise that the Spirit has quickened to us, we can contend for it as surely as the woman in Christ's parable continued to make her claims heard before the unjust judge. Her importunity prevailed, and she was granted her heart's desire.

Praying the Scriptures and identifying with the prayers in the Scriptures will help us learn the difference between personal prayer, public prayer and prayer for others. Sometimes I hear prayers prayed in public that would better have been prayed in private.

Some things should be known only by God who sees in secret. The public has a great curiosity about private affairs. God forgives and forgets, but few people in the church have attained this grace.

Other matters, when prayed publicly, spur fellow-Christians to identify with us; these prayers bring a great release into their spirits. As we pray God's Word, we learn what to say, where to say it and when to refrain from saying it.

Praying the Scriptures helps us to associate with prayer

I was raised in a religious environment that encouraged entire congregations to pray aloud at the same time. It has never bothered me, but people who are unaccustomed to it sometimes find it confusing. They love to point to Paul's teaching that we should take turns in public expression (see 1 Corinthians 14:26). They feel that only one should vocalise the prayer while others identify with that prayer.

I have lived long enough to see value in both positions. Prayer, to be meaningful, requires expression. Praying along with others personally involves us with God and allows us to enjoy the support of a chorus of voices around us.

On the other hand, there are times when one person can best express what the Spirit wants to say while the congregation of believers blends their wills and attitudes with that prayer. I could not begin to count the times when I've sensed that joining the prayer of another has lifted my own prayer to a higher level of communication with God.

The secret of true identification with public prayer is listening closely. Good communicators are good listeners. Their minds are not wandering, looking for answers while the question is being asked; they listen intently to the words, the inflection and the attitude; they watch the body language of the person who is talking to them. Blending with a public prayer requires the same measure of concentration.

If the vocalised prayer expresses some of the deep feelings in the heart, we do well to say 'Amen!' either inwardly or outwardly, depending on what is accepted in the religious circle. How often I have heard myself whisper, 'Yes, Lord! Me, too, Lord!' while another was praying. I couldn't have said it better myself. Frequently, I have the same experience when reading the Scriptures devotionally. The prayers in God's Word often express feelings I have not yet learned to communicate.

Amen! as used in the Bible fundamentally means 'be it so'. Sometimes I substitute the more modern expression *OK!* which simply indicates that we agree with what has been stated. Perhaps we will identify more completely with the prayers of another when we are able to say an honest 'Amen!' to what they are praying.

Every time we pray the Scriptures, we are merely responding to what another has said. When that 'another' is God himself, our 'Amen!' or 'OK' agrees with what he has said and gives him permission to do in our lives what he has expressed a desire to do.

The best prayers have already been prayed, and many of them are recorded in God's Word. If we can learn to incorporate them into our praying, we will greatly expand our prayer lives.

Beyond this, we will begin to rise above the religious tone so often associated with prayer and develop a variety of intonations in expressing our hearts to God.

15

Praying the Scriptures gives intonation to our prayer

Many preachers have a special tone of voice reserved for praying. Some even shift into an unnatural vocabulary. This sometimes suggests a professional approach to talking with God, and it is difficult to believe that Jesus or Paul developed these mannerisms. I expect that they communicated with the heavenly Father very much as they communicated with earthly friends.

Prayer is far more meaningful if it is natural communication. The use of old-English vocabulary doesn't enhance our praying. It is more apt to detract from prayer's effectiveness, as such language is usually unnatural to the speaker. If prayer isn't meaningful to the person praying, it is wasted. God is not impressed by our vocabularies or our understanding of the King James English. He is looking for people who will worship him in spirit and in truth (see John 4:23).

Being natural in prayer, however, involves a lot more than using the vocabulary of everyday speech. The person who is genuinely communicating with God in prayer will vary voice inflection, intonation and volume levels just as in natural speech. The person announcing that the building is on fire uses a different intonation and volume of voice than the person directing you to the recreation room. Similarly, the 'voice' of our prayer will be governed by the nature of the message and the urgency of the situation.

Sometimes I receive a phone call from a person who speaks with such monotone that I'm tempted to hang up without hearing the entire message. But then other speakers have such melodious, pleasant voices that I listen intently to their every word.

I wonder if God feels similarly when listening to us pray. Some prayers express so little emotion it must seem as if a written message is being read from a boiler-room phone operation somewhere on earth. Other people have learned to express their love for God melodiously and to lay their requests pleasantly before him.

I suspect that God responds to each prayer according to the nature of the speaker. If the dull prayer comes from a person whose speech is consistently colourless, I'm certain that God accepts it as a normal offering. However, when the person with a naturally sparkling voice prays a monotonous prayer, God must feel as if he is not sufficiently important to motivate this person to expend the energy that charismatic communication requires.

Repeatedly, the Psalms speak of lifting up the soul to God. David said: 'To you, O Lord, *I lift up my soul.* You are forgiving and good, O Lord, abounding in love to all who call to you. Hear my prayer, O Lord; listen to my cry for mercy' (Psalm 86:4-6).

Perhaps he was only using a poetic expression for prayer, but it does sound as if he was communicating with God with feeling. We know this would be consistent with David, for he often expressed himself to God melodiously. One of his favourite ways to pray was through song.

The overflow of the Word produces song

Paul was a man whose heart was filled with the Word of God, and he consistently urged the converts, over whom he exercised an apostleship, to keep their lives full of the Word. He also taught that the person whose heart is full of Scripture will have a life filled with song.

To the Colossian church he wrote: 'Let the word of Christ dwell in you richly as you teach and admonish one another with all wisdom, and as you sing psalms, hymns and spiritual songs with gratitude in your hearts to God' (Colossians 3:16). Paul was convinced that *song* is the point of overflow for the Word of God.

Whether we realise it or not, we do teach and admonish one another with hymns and spiritual songs. It has well been said that the average Christian learns more doctrine from the hymnbook than from the Bible. What we sing together makes a deeper impression on our minds than what we merely read together. Furthermore, we are more apt to get involved personally with a song than with a Scripture portion.

Advertisers long ago learned and capitalised on the teaching power of song. Unfortunately the church hasn't always been that wise. We have too often taught our children to sing, 'Climb, climb up sunshine mountain' (whatever that is supposed to mean), rather than teaching them to sing God's Word.

From time to time God visits his people with a new wave of his presence, and often the initial response to that move is to sing the Scripture. During the early days of the charismatic renewal, people loved to sing the Scriptures. I then probably learned more verses of God's Word by singing them than I had ever learned by pure rote. More than that, when we sang the Scriptures together as a congregation, we not only shared another's experience, as is common in song; we found ourselves talking directly to God about God, and this is the highest level of prayer – adoration.

I have never lost the joy of singing God's Word during prayer time. Often, when on my daily morning walk, I softly sing portions of God's Word to him. It is a two-way communication, as I am singing what he has said right back to him.

On numerous occasions I've been in bogged-down prayer sessions that were revived by the singing of a song. At other times I have found that a prayer could be sung far easier than it could be spoken as prose. The tailor-made vocabulary, the lilt of the music, the rhythm of the cadence, all contributed to move on the congregation until they could identify with the theme of the song. Prayer-songs usually involve the spirit, soul and body of the singer. They are more apt to release our emotions in prayer than mere recitations.

When the ark of the covenant was successfully brought to Jerusalem and placed in the tabernacle prepared for it, 'David first committed to Asaph and his associates this psalm of thanks to the Lord: "Give thanks to the Lord, call on his name; make known among the nations what he has done. Sing to him, sing praise to him; tell of all his wonderful acts" ' (1 Chronicles 16:7-9).

On such an auspicious occasion when a prayer of thanksgiving was so much in order, David called for that prayer to be uttered in song; the chief musicians of his realm lifted this anthem of praise melodiously to the Lord in front of all Israel.

The overflow of the Spirit produces song

I have never understood why so many Spirit-filled Christians assume that speaking in tongues is the overflow of the Spirit. Yes, it is an evidence of the Spirit's presence in the believer. But Paul taught that singing to the Lord was the point of overflow for the indwelling Spirit of God.

He wrote, 'Do not get drunk on wine, which leads to debauchery. Instead, be filled with the Spirit. Speak to one another with psalms, hymns and spiritual songs. Sing and make music in your heart to the Lord' (Ephesians 5:18-19).

In an earlier book, *Elements of Worship*, I wrote:

'Paul equated the presence of the Spirit with music in the believer.... To Paul, it seemed impossible to be filled with the Spirit and the Word of God without also being filled with song, for the Spirit is a singing Spirit, and God's Word is our hymnbook.

'God's presence and his precepts stir such inward rejoicing that only singing can release it. Paul was more than propounding a theory; he was writing from experience, for some years prior to this letter, he and Silas, while bound in stocks in the inner dungeon at Philippi, had found both emotional and physical release in singing. Paul knew that the Spirit does not sing only in cheerful, happy circumstances, but that the song of the Spirit is consistent in spite of our situation in life.

'Frankly, we need the inner song of the Spirit more in harsh circumstances than in pleasant ones, for song renews faith and courage in the midst of adversity. Song joins us in fellowship with God and others and brings us back to a God-consciousness.

'Singing can give us endurance spiritually, emotionally and physically. How marvellous it is that God's Spirit within us is a singing Spirit.

'Music is, indeed, intrinsic to the believer. We have a song within us – a song born of the Holy Spirit. We need not go through life with a Sony Walkman and earphones, for our music is within us, not without us. Those who have not surrendered their lives to Christ Jesus must depend upon an outside stimulus for their musical inspiration, but Christians have a song deep in their own spirit, and a Saviour who is the consistent theme of that song. The overflow of our spiritual joy explodes into song, and we are comforted, unified and motivated by great gospel singing.'

Since song is resident in the heart of the believer, it should be utilised during prayer time. It is unfair to express ourselves melodiously one to another and insist upon limiting our communication to God to didactic conversation. God loves singing. The God within us is a singing Spirit. We should sing about him, sing to him and let him sing within us when we are communicating with him in the prayer channel.

This overflow in prayer produces intonation

Webster's dictionary defines *intonation* as: 'the manner of singing, playing, or uttering tones: the rise and fall in pitch of the voice in speech'.

Old Testament worshippers were encouraged to worship with intonation, and prayer is but one form of worship. The psalmist cried: 'Sing to the Lord a new song, for he has done marvellous things.... Shout for joy to the Lord, all the earth, burst into jubilant song with music; make music to the Lord with the harp, with the harp and the sound of singing, with trumpets and the blast of the ram's horn – shout for joy before the Lord, the King' (Psalm 98:1, 4-6).

Throughout the whole Bible communication with God was often melodious, and it needs to be melodious in our current experience with God.

I have discovered that prayers of praise, worship and adoration can more easily be expressed melodiously than in a speaking voice. I love to sing my feelings about the Lord to the Lord. Some call this singing in the Spirit, while others refer to it as the song of the Lord. To me, it is simply praying with musical tones that help to release my emotions to God. Paul simply calls it 'sing and make music in your heart to the Lord' (Ephesians 5:19).

This melodious praying is not so much requesting as it is rejoicing. It has moved beyond petition to praise. It is the response of a heart that has transferred its focus from self to God. We sing not to get from God but to give to him. The rejoicing of life cannot find acceptable release in mere words; it must be sung to God.

On several occasions, the Scriptures encourage us to 'sing to the Lord a new song' (Isaiah 42:10; Psalm 33:3; 40:3; 98:1). When I can't call to mind a song that expresses how I feel, I make one up. It need not be a musical masterpiece. As long as it expresses the rejoicing in my soul or the longing of my spirit, it is useful in my prayer life.

Do you want to release inner emotions? Try taking a portion of Scripture and making up a tune to fit it. The words are inspired, and if the melody releases those words as a prayer, this new song has become a useful tool in your prayer arsenal. It is a 'new song' that God urges you to sing to him. It doesn't matter that no-one else will ever hear your song or that no-one will ever join in singing it with you. You are singing it to the Lord, and he enjoys it thoroughly.

Prayer can be as monotonous as a dripping tap or as melodious as a babbling brook. The difference is not the content but the method of expression. When we bring the Scriptures into our praying, we are inspired to bring music, song, dance and even laughter into our communication with God. What an improvement!

When we allow the Scriptures to break us out of the standard religious mold of prayer, we find not only channels to release the rejoicing in our hearts; we also find a new intensity in our praying.

16

Praying the Scriptures gives intensity to our prayer

Do we Christians actually realise that prayer is the number-one purpose and use of the Scriptures? Preaching is not the strongest and greatest purpose for the Word. Although the Bible has many uses, prayer is its highest design and authority. The Bible is first and foremost a prayer book.

This was clearly demonstrated when 'the Word became flesh and made his dwelling among us' (John 1:14). Christ's behaviour was a constant demonstration of the priority God places on prayer. Everything he did was done through prayer. Christ declared that he did nothing of himself.

In the Gospel of John, Jesus is recorded as having said that the words he spoke were the words he heard his Father speak. The works he did were the works he saw his Father do (see John 8:28-29). He refused to exercise his own will, choosing, rather, to do the will of the Father. Jesus was constantly dependent on his Father, and his dependency required a consistent contact with the Father through the prayer channel.

All Christ's great steps, his mighty works, his majestic words and even his choice of disciples were the results of answered prayer. He began his Messianic ministry at the Jordan with prayer and ended his work on the cross with prayer. He died as he lived – praying. His was a life of prayer.

If an artist painted a portrait of Christ, it has never been found. The only picture we have of Jesus is the word picture painted by the Gospel writers, and they picture him praying. Luke pictures Christ in prayer seven times and the other Gospel writers aren't far behind. He arose early to pray. He went to the mountains and quiet resorts to pray. He practised what he taught concerning prayer and he also taught what he had practised.

The Bible teaches us that Christ's ministry was threefold – prophet, priest and king. The prophetic kingly office of Jesus flowed out of his priestly ministry. Jesus prayed everything into being as God's priest and intercessor. He openly walked into it in his earthly ministry.

The prophet looked out, but the priest prayed through. Prayer became the reign and authority over his prophetic and kingly work. Christ saw prayer as his highest work. It was during prayer that he was creative – in the highest sense.

If the ministry of the living Word was first and foremost a ministry of prayer, wouldn't the written Word follow that same pattern? The great mystery of prayer is that it really has its origin in God. Prayer is the very nature of the triune God. Therefore, to understand prayer and to pray effectively, we must get God's own view of prayer. Only the Scriptures can give us an adequate view of prayer as God sees it, and they do it most effectively.

The Scriptures elaborate prayer

Before Jesus ascended into heaven to take his position as our interceding high priest, he instructed his disciples to return to the upper room and tarry until they received power 'from on high' (see Luke 24:49).

They were elated that Jesus was risen from the dead, and they were about to witness his victorious ascension into heaven, but Jesus told them there was more to come. 'Go to the place of prayer!' was the substance of his command.

It doesn't take knowledge of the original Greek language to discover a high level of 'upper room' prayer ministry all the way through the twenty-eight chapters of the book of Acts. This book of Acts is frequently called the 'Acts of the Holy Spirit', while other people have pointed out that the first verse ties the book to the preceding acts of Jesus as recorded in the Gospel of Luke – making this book the continuing 'Acts of Christ'.

Both views are valid, but, actually, this book chronicles the actions of men and women who followed Jesus in his priestly ministry of prayer. Like Jesus, these believers prayed their next steps and actions into being. Everything that transpires in this book happens as the result of prayer. They knew what today's impotent Christians desperately need to learn: Power and prayer always go together. Intercession in prayer is God's own mighty method of operation on earth.

How we need to be aware of the common delusion that God will do on earth what he wants to do whether we pray properly or not!

Nothing is further from the teaching of the Scriptures. God has limited his action to our praying. While it is true that 'the Sovereign Lord does nothing without revealing his plan to his servants the prophets' (Amos 3:7), God's prophets must first be praying people.

As with Abraham, of whom God said, 'Shall I hide from Abraham what I am about to do?' (Genesis 18:17), God reveals his will to inspire our intercession, for God will not do apart from intercession what he has promised to do by it. It is important that we search the Scriptures to find out what God's will is.

'But,' you may counter, 'prayer isn't everything!'

That's true, but, with God, everything is by prayer. Remember Paul's words to the Christians in Philippi: 'Do not be anxious about anything, but in everything, by prayer and petition, with thanksgiving, present your requests to God. And the peace of God, which transcends all understanding, will guard your hearts and your minds in Christ Jesus' (Philippians 4:6-7)?

He doesn't say, 'in emergencies'. He clearly says 'in everything, by prayer and petition'. Our human pride still feels that it is capable of doing something, but the Scriptures teach that there is absolutely *nothing* we are able to do that has spiritual value to it. Everything must be accomplished by prayer.

Because this is true, and because it is so important to God to have a prayer channel through which he can reveal his purposes and release his power, the Scriptures inaugurate our praying. Far too often, we struggle with problem-solving when we should be praying about that problem.

Habakkuk, an Old Testament prophet, found this to be true in his life. In chapter one of his book, he wrestles with the problem of God's apparent disinterest in the current national emergency. He charges God with unfairness and he even suggests that God may be violating his very nature by allowing heathen countries to violate Israel. His great arguments are strong and show a good theological training, but God ignores the prophet's complaints. God doesn't answer theological disputations; he answers prayer.

Habakkuk changes his stance in chapter two. It begins: 'I will stand at my watch and station myself on the ramparts; I will look to see what he will say to me, and what answer I am to give to this complaint' (Habakkuk 2:1). The prophet stopped worrying about national problems and went to prayer. 'Then the Lord replied . . .' (v2), the prophet admitted.

Our finite minds can never comprehend the infinite God, but our anointed spirits can communicate with him. In God's answer to Habakkuk, he let the prophet see the events from a heavenly point of view and then he gave him promises of divine intervention in God's own time.

Habakkuk closed his short prophecy with an intercessory prayer: 'Lord, I have heard of your fame; I stand in awe of your deeds, O Lord. Renew them in our day, in our time make them known; in wrath remember mercy' (Habakkuk 3:2).

Having seen circumstances through God's eyes, the prophet was able to pray the desires of God's heart. Habakkuk could conclude with a benediction of rejoicing: 'Though the fig-tree does not bud and there are no grapes on the vines, though the olive crop fails and the fields produce no food, though there are no sheep in the pen and no cattle in the stalls, yet I will rejoice in the Lord, I will be joyful in God my Saviour. The Sovereign Lord is my strength; he makes my feet like the feet of a deer, he enables me to go on the heights' (Habakkuk 3:17-19).

This shift from problem-solving to prayer is still accomplished by paying attention to what God is saying, and his voice is in his Word. Perhaps we, like Habakkuk, need to exchange mental exercises for communication with God. When we see God's viewpoint, we can pray with his desires. How this would invigorate our prayers!

The Scriptures invigorate prayer

Unspecific prayer is usually lifeless prayer. If we don't know where we are going, we won't recognise when we arrive, so we just aimlessly wander in the prayer circuit hoping that something good will happen.

We have all prayed those dull, non-directive, uninteresting prayers that accomplish nothing. This is not God's will for us. Prayers can be animated and very much alive if we bring the Scriptures into our praying.

There are at least four reasons why praying the Scriptures will invigorate our communication with God. The first reason is that as we incorporate the Scriptures into our praying, we discover the nature of prayer and its importance to the purposes of God and his plan for our lives. Instead of viewing prayer as an interruption of God, we learn that prayer is the link that releases God's plans into life's programmes.

Prayer that enables us to be 'God's fellow-workers' (2 Corinthians 6:1) joins God's purposes. In prayer, we are not so much pleading with God to do for us, as we are making ourselves available for him to do in and through us according to his sovereign will. This will stimulate our praying and fill us with life and energy, for we are involved in the purposes and processes of God's will.

A second reason why using the Scriptures during our prayer animates our praying is because God's Word is the expression of his will. Why does the Scripture say of Jesus, 'I desire to do your will, O my God' (Psalm 40:8; Hebrews 10:7)? Because he knew his Father's will. This knowledge was not his because he was the Son of God, for he had laid aside all his divine prerogatives at the incarnation. He discovered the Father's will the same way we do – through prayer.

As we introduce the written Word of God into our praying, we not only discover the Father's will; we declare it. Our prayer rises above pleading to proclaiming, and this excites our spirits. We recognise that we are no longer repeating our own words. We are saying the very words of God who wrote the Scriptures. We have ceased originating the message and have become messengers for Almighty God as we proclaim his will to the entire spirit world. If this doesn't invigorate our praying, it is unlikely that anything will.

The third reason that praying the Scriptures can strengthen our prayers is because the Word we pray is often God's power being released in our prayer channel. We may begin with what seems little more than quotation of Scripture, but when the Holy Spirit joins us and energises our prayer, we become aware of something extraordinary happening. The release of spiritual energy does not have its origin in us.

Out of his experience, King Solomon declared, 'Where the word of a king is, there is power' (Ecclesiastes 8:4 RAV), and we have already seen that: 'The word of God is living and active. Sharper than any double-edged sword' (Hebrews 4:12).

When God speaks, things happen, and he promises: 'So is my word that goes out from my mouth: It will not return to me empty, but will accomplish what I desire and achieve the purpose for which I sent it' (Isaiah 55:11). When this happens, whether God speaks this directly from heaven, representatively through his angels or inspirationally through a quickening of his written Word, our praying should be invigorated.

The fourth way praying the Scriptures can rouse our prayers is this: The portion of the Bible we pray is often God's feelings being expressed through our emotions. We may know how we feel in any given situation, but it may be inaccurate to project those same feelings to God.

Often the Holy Spirit will direct our hearts to a portion of Scripture that lets us feel what God feels. We may pray God's compassion or his love. We may feel his heartache over a prodigal son and we may share his rejoicing over a sinner who has returned home. This is often far beyond our mental association; the Spirit can make the Scriptures so alive that we feel emotionally what God says he feels. On such occasions our praying takes on the fire of God's fervour.

When we pray God's words, 'I have loved you with an everlasting love; I have drawn you with loving-kindness' (Jeremiah 31:3), we not only feel our natural security; we sense some of the depth of his love for us. It fires up our prayers to feel what God is feeling.

The Scriptures ignite prayer

Some praying reminds me of the breakfast conversation I can imagine between a husband and a wife in a stale marriage. She is rambling on about a real or imagined affront, while he is concealed behind a newspaper, grunting an occasional 'Yes, dear.' Neither of them is interested in meaningful communication, and there is no warmth and enthusiasm in anything being said. The talk is more duty than pleasure.

When prayer is just 'doing our duty', it lacks enthusiasm or fire, but when we introduce the Scriptures into our praying, our duty becomes delightful fellowship with God.

The prayers of great intercessors throughout church history were characterised by enthusiasm, feeling and fire. Like Elijah, they found a promise in God's Word, and they prayed that promise with every bit of emotion that they could put into that prayer. God heard and answered them speedily. Perhaps we need to get back into the Word until the joy of the Word gets back into us. Then our prayers will have the fire of true emotion in them.

Sometimes our prayers are kindled out of need; at

other times they are inflamed by deep desire. But the best way to heat cold prayers until there is a pleasing aroma ascending from them is by using the Scriptures in those prayers. This will not only inspire deep emotion; it will bring the praying person into a more glorious intimacy with the God to whom he or she is praying.

17

Praying the Scriptures gives intimacy to our prayer

Sometimes, when my secretary is not on duty, I answer the phone: 'Dr Cornwall's residence. Judson Cornwall speaking.'

'Hello!' someone responds. 'I'm trying to reach Dr Cornwall.'

'This is Judson Cornwall speaking.'

'Oh, ah, I didn't expect to get you. Dr Cornwall, you don't know me, but I know you. I've probably read all your books and have seen you in several conferences. My name is...and I pastor the United Church in....'

Several things are immediately apparent. The person calling didn't expect to talk to me. He expected to talk to my secretary about me. While he had some knowledge about me, I had absolutely no knowledge about him. For him to build a relationship so that he dared to present his petition, he had to spend some time telling me about himself.

So much praying is like this. We expect to talk about God – not talk to him. If he does answer us, we don't know how to respond. Having succeeded in making contact, we are at a loss for words.

And since our relationship is so distant, we spend much of our time telling God about ourselves. It is strictly a business call, and it has its awkward moments.

In contrast to this call, I also receive calls that go something like this: 'Cornwall residence. Dr Cornwall speaking.'

'Hi, Judson, this is Dick.'

'Dick! It's good to hear your voice. How are you?'

There is instant recognition, instant rapport – drawn on an existing relationship. This call may also be a business call, but it will be transacted as an action between friends. God earnestly wants to bring us into such an intimate relationship with himself that our prayers will be like this call, rather than the first one. We have not merely read about God in his Book; we have come into a personal relationship with him that causes us to recognise his voice and also assures us that he knows our voice.

The Scriptures corroborate our relationship with God

When God appeared on Mount Sinai, the children of Israel were awed to the point of terror. At God's command, Moses went up the mountain to receive the commandments from God.

None of us can truly imagine how overwhelming this was – to hear the voice of God. But Moses had heard God speak before, at the burning bush. As a matter of fact, the continual speaking of God during the plagues of Egypt had made Moses become quite comfortable with talking to God.

This must have been reciprocal, for we read, 'The Lord would speak to Moses face to face, as a man speaks with his friend' (Exodus 33:11). God didn't treat Moses as a servant or even as a prophet. God communicated with Moses as a friend, and God's conversation with Moses during this time had developed into an abiding and intimate relationship.

Moses wasn't the first person to be called God's friend. Several hundred years before, God had called Abraham out of Ur of the Chaldeans. The two of them developed such a warm and intimate relationship that the Bible says that Abraham was called 'God's friend' (James 2:23). Their continued communication, which we would now call prayer, had dispelled all strangeness and had bridged the great gap between them, so that they could enjoy one another as friends.

Moses was neither the first person to be called 'God's friend', nor is he the last such person. Jesus told his disciples, 'Greater love has no-one than this, that he lay down his life for his friends. You are my friends if you do what I command. I no longer call you servants, because a servant does not know his master's business. Instead, I have called you friends, for everything that I learned from my Father I have made known to you' (John 15:13-15).

Jesus taught that, when his sacrifice for us is matched by our obedience to what he says, we come into the relationship of 'God's friends'. How this affects our praying! Like Abraham and Moses, we know the God to whom we are speaking, and we are known to God. The purpose of our prayer, then, is not to establish a relationship but to strengthen that relationship.

When we are in prayer, two things often cause us to separate ourselves from his presence: our sense of distance from God and the conviction that we haven't done all that he would have us do. At this point we need to introduce some of the Scripture verses that deal with our relationship to God.

I was ministering to a church group in Canada. The congregation had gone through difficult times, and they had lost their pastor and most of the congregation. They felt their only solution was to disband and sell the property. I pleaded with the leadership to reconsider that decision and to trust God to see them through this rough patch. I pledged my availability to them during this season.

On one occasion, they flew me in to work with them, and while we were praying, their discouragement became so strong that they couldn't even lift their voices above a whisper.

Challenged by the Holy Spirit, I prayed loudly, 'How great is the love the Father has lavished on us, that we should be called children of God! And that is what we are! The reason the world does not know us is that it did not know him. Dear friends, now we are children of God, and what we will be has not yet been made known. But we know that when he appears, we shall be like him, for we shall see him as he is' (1 John 3:1-2).

This passage of Scripture, prayed by the Spirit of God through me, sparked this handful of people in the most amazing fashion. Instead of approaching God as failures, they prayed as sons and daughters of God. This fresh awareness of their position gave them new boldness in their petition.

God met them, and the church has known dynamic growth in the years since then. They now have new facilities that are probably one thousand per cent larger than previously, but they are no more sons and daughters of God in their bigness than they were in their smallness.

The Scriptures confirm our companionship with God

Ten times a year, my sister, Iverna Tompkins, and I join forces in conducting special training sessions for a small select group of ministers. Quite consistently I conduct the early morning hour of prayer during which I strive to teach the ministers how to use this tool of prayer in their daily lives. Quite often someone asks me, 'How can I learn to pray with the intimacy I hear in the others?'

The answer is, 'We all pray our relationship. If our relationship is intimate, we can pray intimately.'

If prayer were just vocalising the needs, the relationship would be unimportant, but prayer is the communication of our spirits with God's Spirit. In our natural lives, the level at which we speak to one another is determined by the relationship that exists between the speakers. Strangers talk about the weather or TV programmes. Partners talk about business. Acquaintances may talk about common friends or family members, while friends often talk about feelings and problems.

Probably the most intimate communication is reserved for those who have developed a companionship with each other. Just as I speak more intimately with my wife than I do with any other woman, so my relationship with God establishes the intimacy level of my prayer.

While in prayer I might feel quickened to cry out, 'Come, let us bow down in worship, let us kneel before the Lord our Maker; for he is our God and we are the people of his pasture, the flock under his care' (Psalm 95:6-7).

Almost immediately I will sense a companionship with God. 'We are the people of his pasture, the flock under his care.' If we are his sheep, then he is our shepherd. His responsibility is to lead; ours is to follow. In this relationship he provides the pasture, the water and the protection for us, and we provide wool and lambs for him. It is a two-way relationship and it deeply affects the way we pray.

If we feel quickened to pray, 'They will be called, "sons of the living God" ' (Hosea 1:10; Romans 9:26), our prayer takes on the intimacy of a father-son talk. As children, we are not expected to know everything, but we expect our Father to have all the answers.

Children are submissive under the training of their fathers, and they exercise very few rights of their own. Children live under the security of parental love, and so do God's children.

When we pray out of the parent-child relationship, we communicate an intimacy that no-one outside the family circle will ever experience. We share his name; we possess some of his nature; we are part of the sum of the family secrets.

All our awareness of our companionship with God comes from the Scriptures. As we use them in prayer, our relationship with God proceeds from knowing 'that there is a God in Israel' (1 Samuel 17:46) to letting 'the favour of the Lord our God rest upon us' (Psalm 90:17). We can call him 'our' God instead of 'a' God, much as Samson's 'O Sovereign God' (Judges 16:28) was elevated to Ethan's 'You are my Father, my God' (Psalm 89:26).

The more personal the relationship becomes, the more intimate the prayer will be. Our awareness of that intimacy determines the level of our communication. Since our human nature cannot be trusted, we dare not lean on our own understanding concerning our relationship with God. We need to trust the clear, unmistakable teaching of the Scriptures. What they declare our relationship to be already exists. Our speaking doesn't produce that relationship; it practices it.

We can communicate to God out of these companion relationships and know that we will be accepted by God, for God has declared, 'I will not violate my covenant or alter what my lips have uttered' (Psalm 89:34). The more we incorporate the Scriptures into our praying, the warmer our communication with God will be.

The Scriptures certify our authority with God

In teaching members of my congregation how to pray, I invited them to join me in my morning prayer time, and occasionally I secretly recorded their praying. A few days later, I invited them to my study and played a portion of the tape to them. It never made me popular, but it was a tremendous revelation to them as to what they sounded like when they prayed.

Some prayers were apologies while others sounded like a nagging whine. Some were a meaningless collection of religious phrases and clichés mixed with a vast quantity of information they felt God should know about. Only a God of great patience would bother to listen to these prayers.

After the moans and groans had subsided (and the charges of invasion of privacy had been settled by my giving them the tape and assuring them that I had played it only this once, in their presence), I talked to them about praying with authority.

Repeatedly, Jesus gave us the authority 'in my name'. His name is our power of attorney to do business on his behalf. That name is well-respected in heaven, on earth and in hell. When we function in that confirmed authority, things happen. Mark ends his Gospel with the words of Jesus: 'In my name they will drive out demons; they will speak in new tongues; they will pick up snakes with their hands; and when they drink deadly poison, it will not hurt them at all; they will place their hands on sick people, and they will get well' (Mark 16:17-18).

Our authority is at least threefold. First, we have been authorised to request of God in Jesus' name. Second, we have been empowered to rebuke demons in Jesus' name. Third, we have been commissioned to relieve people from their afflictions. This is an authority in heaven, on earth and over hell. This makes for some very dynamic praying.

There is an inherent danger in seeking to exercise this authority. It is an authority that comes out of an intimate relationship with God. If we are going to do business in that name, we must bear that name. My wife can transact business in my name because she has carried that name in marriage for over forty-six years. There is a danger in assuming that because we have learned a formula, we can make it work. No prayer will have power and authority if the intimate relationship with God has been broken.

It is not the words that have been spoken but the power that stands behind those words that gives them such authority. The policeman in uniform is obeyed not because he is older, wiser or even stronger, but because the enforcement power of the entire nation stands behind him. His uniform and badge give weight to his words because they speak of his legal authority. Similarly, when our relationship with Christ shows in our praying, the authority of heaven stands behind our words, and the 'all authority' that was given to Jesus (see Matthew 28:18) stands behind our praying.

When Peter and John spoke a word of healing to the lame man at the temple gate which was called Beautiful, Peter said to him, 'In the name of Jesus Christ of Nazareth, walk' (Acts 3:6). This miracle drew such a large crowd that Peter was called upon to explain what had happened. His answer to their 'How?' was: 'By faith in the name of Jesus, this man whom you see and know was made strong' (Acts 3:16).

This led to Peter's arrest, and the next day, when the rulers, elders and scribes, as well as the high priest Annas, questioned Peter, his explanation was simply: 'Know this, you and all the people of Israel: It is by the name of Jesus Christ of Nazareth, whom you crucified but whom God raised from the dead, that this man stands before you healed' (Acts 4:10).

Peter transacted business on Christ's behalf and in his name. That was a high level of prayer as well as an intimate prayer. It is still an available level of prayer, but to be effective it demands the incorporation of the Scriptures into our praying. It involves the authorities of God and what he has said, more than what we feel or need.

Prayer that flows out of our relationship and companionship with God takes on all the authorities given to us in the Scriptures. This prayer is not only powerful; it is perfumed.

It is forceful on earth and a fragrance in heaven.

18

Praying the Scriptures gives incense to our prayer

From the earliest religious cultures until today, incense is and has been an ingredient in worship. It was certainly widely used by the Egyptian priests during Israel's slavery there.

Satan, who is directly or indirectly behind all false worship, received all his training on the job in heaven. So you might expect that fire, smoke and fragrance would be part of false worship, as they are heavenly ingredients of worship. Satan's goal in heaven was to replace God as the object of worship, and it is still his goal here on earth.

Because the burning of incense has become such an integral part of idol worship, the reformers set it aside as an unnecessary ritual in true worship. Some Christian cultures still use it in one way or another, but most have been content to place a spiritual meaning on this outward act, much as the death of Jesus on the cross gave spiritual meaning to the work of the brazen altar. The principle of the New Testament is: 'First the natural, then the spiritual' (see 1 Corinthians 15:46).

These natural symbols are referred to as *types* and the spiritual fulfilment of each is the *antitype*. The Old Testament abounds in types, many of which point directly to the coming of Christ Jesus. They often picture or foreshadow his person, his work, his death, his resurrection and his triumphant ascension.

Incense is sometimes classified as a *type* of Christ, who offered up his life as a sweet-smelling fragrance to the Father. There's no question that the characterisation fits, but it seems to me that incense is equally a clear picture of a believer's life poured out before the Father in high-level prayer. Incense and worship are still inseparable.

Incense in tabernacle prayer

The Mosaic tabernacle in the wilderness was constructed exactly as God designed it, and all the worship followed the pattern that God gave to Moses on the mountain.

All the rituals were to enable the people to approach a living God. There were patterns of ritual for the people to follow, higher forms of ritual for the Levitical priests, while the highest forms of worship were reserved for the Aaronic priesthood. Rituals extended from offering to God a common sparrow on the brazen altar of the outer court to burning incense on the golden altar in the holy place.

The burning of incense had nothing to do with making atonement for sin, which always required a blood sacrifice. Incense was not connected with the petitions of the people or the intercessions of the priests, which were normally accompanied by feasting, fasting or peace offerings.

Incense was burned exclusively for God. The golden altar was placed directly in front of the veil that divided the tent tabernacle in half. The clouds of smoke produced by the burning incense filled both the priestly compartment and the holiest of holies where God's throne resided. Priests burned incense as an act of worship to bring the attention of the priest from the needs of the people to the presence of Almighty God. This fragrance was never smelled outside the holy place, except for the short-lived odour that lingered on the garments of the priests who had been in God's presence.

The incense was compounded in equal measurements of four sweet spices: stacte (gum resin), onycha, galbanum and pure frankincense. God had said, 'Make a fragrant blend of incense, the work of a perfumer. It is to be salted and pure and sacred.... Do not make any incense with this formula for yourselves; consider it holy to the Lord' (Exodus 30:35, 37).

When the priest entered the holy place to tend to the lampstand, he was to take a handful of incense and throw it on the coals of the golden altar, signifying that all service done in the presence of God must be done in an atmosphere of worship. This was also done on the day of atonement when the high priest went through the veil into God's throne room with the basin of blood in one hand and a golden censer, filled with incense, in the other hand.

From the very beginning, God taught that the closer we come to his presence, the more important worship becomes.

However, this worship, in the holy place, was not totally disconnected from the purging of sin in the outer court; the hot coals upon which the incense was burned were brought in daily from the outer brazen altar. Worship can never be totally separated from the work of the cross. Until sin is a settled issue, we dare not approach a holy God. When we do approach him with the incense of praise, worship and adoration, our approach is ignited by the finished work of Jesus Christ at Calvary. Unless the fire of this costly sacrifice burns within our hearts, no clouds of incense will billow up from our lives into God's presence.

Every ritual in the tabernacle in the wilderness was necessary. If size determines importance, then the brazen altar was the most important, for it was large enough to hold all the other pieces of tabernacle furniture. This would make the golden altar the least valuable, for it was the smallest of all the furniture.

If proximity to God determined the value, then the golden altar of incense, which was the closest a priest could come to God without going through the veil, was the most valuable. If meeting the needs of people approaching God determines significance, then the station of worship that met those needs was the most important.

All pieces of furniture in the tabernacle were necessary to prepare the person for the presence of God. Their use was progressive, and the goal was to get to God.

Similarly, there are ascending levels of prayer taught in the Scriptures. The lowest level of prayer is that of *confession,* which deals with sin, while the highest level is *adoration,* which deals exclusively with God. Every level of prayer has its place, just as every ritual in the tabernacle in the wilderness was necessary. In prayer, we proceed from our sinful condition to a place where we can worship and adore God for himself alone.

When prayer reaches beyond our personal need to the person of God, it becomes incense that blesses God and brings us into his presence. Prayer, as incense, is totally impossible without the ingredient of the Scriptures.

Incense in today's prayer

When John the beloved was caught into heaven, he twice saw how incense was used in the worship of God. The first time was when 'the four living creatures and the twenty-four elders fell down before the

Lamb. Each one had a harp and they were holding golden bowls full of incense, which are the prayers of the saints' (Revelation 5:8).

John saw the fulfilment of the Old Testament type in this heavenly worship. Incense is the prayer of the saints, and they are entrusted to these high-level creatures of heaven and the redeemed elders of earth.

The second time John saw incense was when Christ opened the seventh seal, causing silence in heaven for about half an hour. He described the scene:

'I saw the seven angels who stand before God, and to them were given seven trumpets. Another angel, who had a golden censer, came and stood at the altar. He was given much incense to offer, with the prayers of all the saints, on the golden altar before the throne. The smoke of the incense, together with the prayers of the saints, went up before God from the angel's hand' (Revelation 8:2-4).

Although this angel isn't identified, the fact that he has a golden censer would place him among the 'four living creatures' of Revelation 5. As he presents the prayers of the saints before the throne of God, there seems to be a missing ingredient. The fragrance is wrong, so 'he was given much incense to offer, with the prayers of all the saints, on the golden altar before the throne'. Our interceding high priest, Jesus, mixes his perfect prayers with the imperfect prayers of the saints on earth so that the fragrance will have the proper balance by the time it gets to the nostrils of God. On earth, the written Word becomes the frankincense; in heaven, it is the living Word, Christ Jesus, who becomes the activator, the one who produces the smoke that adds the final odour to the fragrance.

This is the way worship is offered to God in eternity. Our prayers, insufficient and selfish as they may be, are mixed with the perfect prayers of Jesus

Christ and presented to God in such a blend as to have the correct aroma for heaven's atmosphere. The written Word together with the living Word makes certain that our incensed prayers bring pleasure to God and to all around the throne of God in heaven.

Our prayers, then, are not restricted to the planet Earth or to the capsule of time. Our prayers are gathered from earth and presented in heaven, where they are mixed with the eternal Word of God and presented to the eternal God as a perfect blend of heaven and earth. When we pray the Scriptures, we enter into a high level of intercession where our praying is mingled with the prayers of Christ Jesus.

19

Praying the Scriptures gives intercession to our prayer

Because vocabulary not only expresses concepts but also forms those concepts in our minds, I approach any teaching on intercession with caution.

The popular usage of the word *intercession* has made a noun out of a scriptural verb; people are referred to as *intercessors* rather than as those who engage in intercessory prayer. Scripturally, Jesus is the only person given the title and office of intercessor. Many other people offer prayers of intercession, but only Jesus is called the intercessor. Paul clearly taught, 'There is one God and one mediator between God and men, the man Christ Jesus' (1 Timothy 2:5). This gives Christ the divine monopoly of the office of intercessor.

In the exercise of this office, Jesus uses a variety of channels through which the ministry of intercession is activated. He uses the Scriptures to intercede with us; he uses us to intercede with one another; he uses the indwelling Spirit to intercede through us on behalf of others.

If we make an office out of the ministry, we will limit the channels available to Christ for the exercise of his office of intercessor. He can, and very likely will, intercede through each praying person at one time or another. We don't need a special calling, special training or special titles to be a channel for divine intercession. We need only to heed the Holy Spirit's call to prayer. We don't initiate intercession; we participate in it. We don't even choose the person or the situation for which we will intercede. The Spirit will make that choice.

In its purest scriptural sense, intercession is putting one's self in the place of others and, in prayer, strongly identifying with them in their need. Only the Holy Spirit can produce this in us. We may initiate a prayer on a subject or situation and then sense that the Spirit moves us from petition to intercession, but until he moves to intercede through us, we cannot pray the prayer of intercession.

Over the years I have broadened my concept of intercessory prayer to embrace prevailing and travailing prayer. Whether this is important or not may depend on the importance one places on semantics.

Using this broadened concept, one might say that intercessory prayer interposes, intervenes, intermediates and interacts. It *interposes* the person praying. It *intervenes* on behalf of the person for whom the prayer is offered. It *intermediates* for a solution, and it *interacts* to perform what is necessary for the resolution of the problem or the fulfilment of God's promises. God's Word is a beautiful channel of intercession in all four of these ways.

The Scriptures intercede *with us* to pray

Long before the Scriptures intercede through us in prayer, they intercede with us to pray. Just as my computer can't do word processing until I call up the word processing software, we can't intercede unless we are in the prayer mode. Sometimes the Holy Spirit urges our spirits to step aside from our activities and spend time seeking the face of the

Lord. Then, once we come into God's presence, we may feel a burden of intercession laid upon us.

At other times the Spirit works through the Scriptures, which intercede with us to pray. While reading in the Word, we may come upon a passage that says, "Let us go at once to entreat the Lord and seek the Lord Almighty. I myself am going.' And many peoples and powerful nations will come...to seek the Lord Almighty and to entreat him' (Zechariah 8:21-22).

The simple reading of the Scripture becomes a personal intercession of God to bring us to prayer. The Holy Spirit quickens and illuminates the passage to our hearts; it seems that God is putting this very cry in our spirits. We find ourselves challenged to pray, even though we had not planned to pray.

We may read of Paul saying, 'We have not stopped praying for you' (Colossians 1:9), and, 'Pray continually' (1 Thessalonians 5:17), and be challenged to maintain an attitude of prayer throughout the day. Although our conscious minds may be occupied with many affairs, our spirits are free to reach out to God continually. This keeps us prepared so that the Spirit can intercede through us at a moment's notice.

Mature Christians have learned that God never commands us to do without first enabling us to do. If God says, 'Pray without ceasing,' he enables us to stay in the prayer mode.

Furthermore, the Scriptures intercede with us to pray by helping us to see what God sees. Though the Spirit occasionally calls believers to intercede for the unknown, it is far more likely that God through his Word will unveil something for which he wants us to intercede. It may be a grace he wishes to perfect in a person for whom we have been praying; it may be for a work that God desires to do in the community.

Whenever we can see circumstances through the eyes of God, we are far more likely to pray about them with the heart of God and according to the revealed will of God. Much of our praying remains selfish because we see things through the eyes of self, but when the Scriptures give us the divine view, we pray from an entirely different perspective.

The Scriptures intercede with us to pray also to convince us that our prayers can make a difference. The constant reassurance of the Word that God hears and responds to our prayers helps keep us in the posture of prayer.

Realistic testimonies of answered prayer have always spurred others to renew their praying. The Bible is full of such testimonies. When we read of God's answering Joshua's prayer for the sun to stand still, or Isaiah's prayer for the sun to go down on the dial as a sign to King Hezekiah, we realise that God does respond to the prayers of people.

In *The Secret of Personal Prayer* I wrote: 'Someone traced 667 prayers for specific things in the Bible and found 454 traceable recorded answers for the prayers – that means nearly seventy per cent. That should settle the question of whether or not God answers prayer!' Then, when the Spirit reminds us that 'Jesus Christ is the same yesterday and today and for ever' (Hebrews 13:8), we are gently nudged to return to our private closet of prayer.

The Scriptures intercede *in us* as we pray

One of the first things we learn when we give ourselves to serious prayer is that we don't know how to pray. Paul wrote: 'The Spirit helps us in our weakness. We do not know what we ought to pray for, but the Spirit himself intercedes for us with groans that words cannot express' (Romans 8:26). This verse is the admission of our inability and the addition of his ability in our praying. When we realise that we can't pray properly, the Scriptures assure us of the presence of God's Spirit, who helps us to pray in at least four ways.

Perhaps the Spirit's first step in intercession with us is to illuminate the Scriptures to our hearts. When writing to the Ephesians, Paul prayed that 'the God of our Lord Jesus Christ, the glorious Father, may give you the Spirit of wisdom and revelation, so that you may know him better. I pray also that the eyes of your heart may be enlightened in order that you may know the hope to which he has called you, the riches of his glorious inheritance in the saints, and his incomparably great power for us who believe. That power is like the working of his mighty strength' (Ephesians 1:17-19).

Paul pleaded with God to open the Scriptures to the saints and to open the eyes of the saints to the Scriptures. This is essential to intercessory prayer.

The Holy Spirit is God's torchbearer. His task is to teach us all things as Jesus promised. He frequently does this by illuminating the Scriptures and enlightening our spiritual understanding to what God has promised. Have you ever read a very familiar portion of Scripture that seemed to light up suddenly like a neon sign? The Spirit quickened the Scripture to your life with new understanding; faith was born in your heart for the fulfilment of that promise. When this happens, prayer takes on a whole new character. We move from petition to intercession, for the Scriptures have joined our praying, producing new faith and confidence.

A second way the Holy Spirit helps our weaknesses in praying is by giving direction to our prayers. When we are deeply engaged in praying about a problem or situation, the Holy Spirit can quicken a promise of God's Word and thereby unlock the will of God before our eyes. He makes the Bible promises come alive and relates them to the situation for which we are praying. When this happens, a conviction is born within us: God will work in that matter – even though the prospect of his doing so may appear to be extremely remote, if not impossible.

Hebrews 11 is filled with the stories of men and women who dared to believe what God said in spite of the impossible odds. They believed God with the faith inspired by the spoken Word of God, and the impossible was fulfilled for them.

A third way the Holy Spirit helps our weaknesses in prayer is to use the Scriptures to give us a revelation of God's will. This is consistent with Paul's prayer that God may give us 'the Spirit of...revelation, so that you may know him better'.

We usually know what our will is when we go to prayer, but we earnestly desire to pray, 'Yet not my will, but yours be done' (Luke 22:42), as Jesus prayed in the garden. If we don't know what his will is, we dangle on the edge of nothing. When our wills have fully surrendered to God, the Spirit delights in opening a portion of the Word that reveals the will of God in the situation for which we have been praying. This releases us to move from submission to intercession in prayer for we are now praying for what we know to be the desire of God in the situation.

The fourth way the Holy Spirit joins us to move our praying into intercession is 'with groans that words cannot express' (Romans 8:26). However we may apply that statement, it fundamentally means that there are deep longings for which we lack sufficient vocabulary to give expression to our feelings. Ken Taylor, in his paraphrased *Living Bible,* translates it: 'The Holy Spirit prays for us with such feeling that it cannot be expressed in words.' Charles Spurgeon quoted Madame Guyon's translation: 'With raptures of ecstasy.'

Whether by illuminating the Scriptures until faith is imparted, directing our prayers into the paths of the Scriptures, revealing God's will in the Scriptures or directly praying through us in an inexpressible way, the Holy Spirit is always the key to true intercession, and his major tool is God's Word.

The Scriptures intercede *through us* as we pray

The initial work of the Spirit is to enable us to intercede according to the will of God. When we have reached the limit of our ability, he often joins us and intercedes through us, perhaps 'with groans that words cannot express,' and, more likely, with a language which we can express as he gives us a vocabulary. Sometimes we comprehend what we are saying. At other times he prays so far beyond our faith levels that we don't grasp what we are saying.

Intercessory prayer speaks to God. It isn't important that a person comprehends what is being said. When I am ministering in Europe, it isn't important for me to understand what my interpreter is saying. Those to whom he is speaking understand him perfectly. The important thing is for the message I am giving to be communicated in a meaningful manner.

It is similar with prayer. The Scriptures teach, 'Anyone who speaks in a tongue does not speak to men but to God. Indeed, no-one understands him; he utters mysteries with his spirit' (1 Corinthians 14:2). Prayer is the most valuable use of tongues, for it is 'speaking to God'.

It has been charged that speaking with tongues is gibberish or, at best, an artificial language, but the Scriptures refer to the language as 'the tongues of men and of angels' (1 Corinthians 13:1). The Holy Spirit is certainly not limited to the English language, nor is he confined to modern languages. He has access to every language ever used by humankind, and he is very familiar with the language used in heaven.

When deep intercession is needed, the Spirit often uses a language that is beyond the intellectual grasp of the speaker to bypass the censorship of his or her conscious mind, thereby enabling the Spirit to say what needs to be prayed without arguing with the faith level of the one through whom the intercession flows.

Praying in tongues is not the work of the sub-conscious. It's really *supra-intellectual* praying. That is, the prayer is beyond the natural mind, not beneath the conscious level. Intercessory prayer in tongues is not incoherent speech. The very words are motivated by the Holy Spirit, addressed to the Father and approved by the Lord Jesus (see Mark 16:17).

The speaker isn't in a trance. The language is spoken with the complete co-operation of the praying person, and the person can stop praying in tongues whenever he or she chooses to do so. The believer knows what he or she is doing when praying in tongues.

Furthermore, intercession of the Spirit in tongues is not *contra-intellectual.* This kind of prayer is neither an overwhelming nor an anti-intellectual experience beyond the control of the person. For the Spirit-filled believer, this kind of intercession is very natural. It allows the Spirit to pray through us intellectually without violating our own intellect.

When describing the whole armour of God that Christians need to wear, the Scriptures say, 'Pray in the Spirit on all occasions with all kinds of prayers and requests' (Ephesians 6:18). This is the same terminology used by Paul in the Corinthian letter: 'If I pray in a tongue, my spirit prays, but my mind is unfruitful. So what shall I do? I will pray with my spirit, but I will also pray with my mind; I will sing with my spirit, but I will also sing with my mind' (1 Corinthians 14:14-15).

Praying 'with all kinds of prayers and requests'

must include praying in tongues, for this is one of the highest levels of intercession by which the Holy Spirit can pray in a New Testament believer. Intercession in tongues is taught in the written Word, activated by the Spirit on earth and directed to the living Word in heaven. It has the three necessary ingredients for intercessory prayer: the authority of the Scriptures, the ability of the Spirit and the avenue of a praying person.

When we allow the Holy Spirit to intercede through us, our prayer joins the intercession of Christ Jesus in heaven and moves us out of our time-space dimension into God's realm of eternity. We are probably closer to immortality during intercessory prayer than during any other occasion.

20

Praying the Scriptures gives immortality to our prayer

The book of beginnings says: 'God created man in his own image, in the image of God he created him; male and female he created them' (Genesis 1:27). This God is called 'the eternal God' (Deuteronomy 33:27), and the New Testament says, 'God has given us eternal life, and this life is in his Son' (1 John 5:11). In sharing his image, God shared his eternity, and in giving his Son, he reinforced this life.

The brilliant King Solomon had some awareness of this, for he wrote: '[God] has...set eternity in the hearts of men' (Ecclesiastes 3:11). There have always been some who seek to deny their immortality, espousing the philosophy, 'Eat, drink and be merry, for tomorrow we may die,' but it is difficult to deny in the head what is alive in the spirit. It is not our faith that puts eternity in our hearts; it is God, and his gift is part of the creation process.

Eternal life, not mere eternal existence, is God's gift to the person who accepts Jesus Christ as Lord. John wrote: 'This is the testimony: God has given us eternal life, and this life is in his Son. He who has the Son has life; he who does not have the Son of God does not have life' (1 John 5:11-12). This is a present-tense experience, and it should not be relocated into the far distant future, after Christ returns and the dead are raised.

Even people who deny the existence of God carry an awareness of immortality, and they use a variety of measures to reach for it. Responding to their inner awareness of eternity, they seek to contact the 'other world,' as they put it. Some try this contact through séances, while many people embrace reincarnation with the belief that the dead merely progress into another form of life – always seeking to ascend – eventually reaching an ultimate assumption into their god. They desperately try to remember what it was like in a previous existence, always wondering what form they will have in the coming life.

Shirley MacLaine has popularised seminars to teach people how to 'channel', that is, to become vessels through which people in other worlds can communicate with people in this world. Satanists have been trying this for years.

Whatever form these attempts to touch eternity may take, they reflect a response to an inner awareness that there is something, or someone, beyond this time-space dimension in which we are imprisoned. Eternity is, indeed, in our hearts, and it rebels at being forced to lie dormant in our spirits. Just as water seeks its own level, so spirit flows to spirit. The psalmist put it: 'Deep calls to deep in the roar of your waterfalls' (Psalm 42:7).

It is the Christian who is able to move from theory and superstition to an actual contact with eternity. The eternal spirits of men and women contact the eternal God through prayer.

God, who placed a measure of his eternal nature in each of us, hasn't totally insulated us from eternity. Time is actually in God's eternity a parenthesis during which God contains rebellion. When all wills are once again subject to the will of God, time will end, and we will step out of the confines of our paren-thesis into the limitlessness of God's eternity.

Scriptural prayer gives victory over hindrances

Attempts to release our eternal spirits to contact God are blocked by hindrances: the uncertainty of the unknown with its incumbent fear; the blindness of extreme world-consciousness with its insensitivity to anything beyond our five basic senses. Added to these difficulties is the indwelling sin which has separated us from God and the arch-enemy who exerts every force at his command to prevent our contacting a living, loving eternal God.

It is self-evident that none of us possesses the inherent power to overcome these obstacles. We are pretty much like the baby in the womb – basically unaware of the other world. When awareness comes to us, we are unable to respond to it until the moment of our birth. We need more than informa-tion; we need transformation. God's Word will inform us, but when we pray those Scriptures, they begin to transform us.

The most obvious hindrance to our contacting God is sin, for it is our sin that has created the great gulf of separation between us and our God. Even after our initial deliverance from the pollution, power and penalty of sin (when we accepted the work of Christ at Calvary as effective in our lives), we continue to battle the presence of sin. Our human nature has a propensity to sin, and the world around us is filled with enticements to sin. Our minds are bombarded repeatedly with sinful images, until our spirits feel as if they are back under the bondage of sin.

When we believers find ourselves re-engaged in a conflict with sin, it is time to bring the Scriptures into our prayers. Sin may entice the believer, but it can't enslave the saint. God's Word affirms, 'Sin shall not be your master' (Romans 6:14). When the initial attempt to contact God in prayer seems thwarted by a consciousness of sin, we need but incorporate the Scriptures into our praying. They will assure us that sin will not dominate us; they also promise us that Christ's blood will cleanse us from every vestige of sin (see 1 John 1:9).

With our unholiness removed, we dare attempt another approach to a holy God, but often we find as much hindrance in our self-life as we had found in sin. Our human thoughts, ambitions, desires and prides, plus the insistent exercise of our personal wills, greatly hinder our contact with God in prayer.

This extreme self-centredness is common to human behaviour, and all Christians are humans. When we recognise the activity of this hindrance to prayer, we need to bring the Scriptures into our praying.

Perhaps we should reaffirm Paul's declaration of identification with Christ: 'I have been crucified with Christ and I no longer live, but Christ lives in me. The life I live in the body, I live by faith in the Son of God, who loved me and gave himself for me' (Galatians 2:20). As this becomes our prayer we can return the control of our lives to the indwelling Christ. Mere attempts to renounce the self-life will fail, but such identification with Christ will bury that life, and that which is dead should not be a great hindrance to the life of prayer.

When we have successfully prayed ourselves beyond the hindrance of sin and self, we should be alerted to the outer interference of the satanic realm. The devil consistently attempts to break our prayer contact with God. His major tool is accusation. He accuses us to God, accuses God to us and even accuses us to ourselves. Our best defence is to accept what the Scriptures have said while totally rejecting everything that the enemy says. After all, the Bible does declare: 'The God of peace will soon crush Satan under your feet' (Romans 16:20).

No matter how loudly this predator may roar, he doesn't have power over the children of God. He has been crushed and rendered powerless to prevent our contact with God. When Satan's lies seem to prevent our prayers from reaching the ceiling of our prayer closets, we need only to pray the declaration of God's Word until our hearts believe God once again.

This same action will deliver us from skepticism that tends to encroach upon us early in our prayer time. When we first pray, seldom do we 'feel' that God hears our prayers. The mind then tends to make us feel foolish, and the soul suggests more worthwhile ways to invest our time. We need the reassurance of God's Word: When we pray, he listens; when we call, he answers. Pray aloud these kinds of Scriptures when your mind questions the validity of your praying.

Praying aloud God's Word can also enable you to battle sleepiness in time of prayer. Had the disciples incorporated the words of Jesus into their praying in the Garden of Gethsemane, they could have remained awake.

E.M. Bounds, a great man of prayer whose books have stirred thousands to more fervent praying, declared that sleepiness in the time of prayer was always a work of the devil. Whether or not this is so may be open to debate, but I and many others can testify that sleepiness seems to follow on the heels of any exercise of prayer. Maybe we need to use what wakeful energy we have to pray, 'Wake up, O sleeper, rise from the dead, and Christ will shine on you' (Ephesians 5:14).

Whether this is a caution, a command or a commitment – it works! I have repeatedly prayed this passage when fighting sleep, and I have discovered the

Holy Spirit using it to energise me to renewed vigour.

There will always be hindrances to prayer, but we have been given powerful tools in the Scriptures to overcome anything and everything that would separate us from God's presence. This is how important prayer is to God. He helps us to make contact with himself.

Scriptural prayer links time and eternity

Prayer is the communication bridge that links heaven and earth and allows time to pierce into eternity. It permits mortal people to fellowship and commune with the immortal God, and it provides him with a channel through which he can communicate with people far removed from his heaven.

If the Scriptures were being written in our generation, I suspect that one of the writers would liken prayer to the communication link between spaceship Earth and home-base heaven. Our origins are in God, and he is our final destination, but for our brief sojourn in this time-space dimension of existence, we are physically separated from God. Through the prayer-link communication, we can maintain a closeness to God's love, wisdom, directions and interventions into our affairs.

When astronauts experience a malfunction of equipment in space, the ground control crew radios a solution to them. Similarly, God makes himself and his solutions available to us on spaceship Earth.

Until Jesus Christ returns and transforms our earthly bodies into spiritual ones, we are earthlings confined to time – or at least two-thirds of our being is time-warped. There is, however, that eternal spirit within us that belongs to eternity. Just as our bodies are uncomfortable in spiritual situations, so our spirits are out of their natural element in this period of time. There is a longing, a groaning, a sighing, even a crying for release from the captivity of earthly bodies. That cry will someday be fulfilled, but, for the present, we can release our spirits into the atmosphere of eternity for brief periods by giving ourselves to prayer.

Paul must certainly have experienced this, for he wrote: 'We ourselves, who have the firstfruits of the Spirit, groan inwardly as we wait eagerly for our adoption as sons, the redemption of our bodies' (Romans 8:23). But while we wait, we need not continuously imprison our spirits. We can release them into the environment of eternity through prayer.

Three times in two connecting psalms, the psalmist cries, 'Why are you downcast, O my soul? Why so disturbed within me? Put your hope in God, for I will yet praise him, my Saviour and my God' (Psalm 42:5, 11; 43:5). How often have I feared that I was at the onset of depression when it was nothing more than my spirit complaining about its confinement. When I gave myself to prayer, my spirit began to rejoice, and my whole being came alive. It wasn't depression. It was oppression of my spirit. My spirit wanted out of its confines for a season of deep breathing of the atmosphere of God in prayer.

Scriptural prayer outlasts time

My personal craving for immortality has driven me to a variety of accomplishments. I have personally supervised the construction of church edifices that will outlast me by many years. I have written books that will probably survive my passing. I rejoice in my three daughters, nine grandchildren and six great-grandchildren. In them, I shall live on after death.

Judson Cornwall will not completely pass away at his funeral. Still, all of these extensions are tied to the same time-space dimension in which I am now a prisoner. They are merely earthly accomplishments. They, too, will pass away.

The only things I have been involved in during my years on earth that will go into eternity ahead of me and survive for ever are the prayers I have prayed in the Spirit. These prayers have reached deep into immortality and have been presented before the throne of God by the mighty angel who has the responsibility to collect the prayers of the saints and mix those prayers with the prayers of Jesus.

When I enter eternity, I will smell the fragrant aroma of heaven. It is beyond description. I know, for I have already smelled it several times. When I wrote my first book, *Let Us Praise*, the room frequently filled with the divine aroma. After gaining entrance to heaven, I will see the clouds of incense and smell its unique blend of fragrances. Then I will know that part of that odour is the prayers I prayed while still travelling on spaceship Earth.

Prayer is the only eternal thing we do while here on earth. Many of our activities affect our eternal life to come, but prayer participates in it right now. When we incorporate the Scriptures into our praying, we not only enter the eternity of our future, but we get involved in the eternity of our past and present, for God's Word is, was and shall always be. We don't fully comprehend God's eternal now, but when we pray his Word, we become involved in it right here on the earth.

Praying the Scriptures is gloriously practical and productive. It is effective in both time and eternity. It affects both God and people. It produces a present fruit of righteousness and a future fruit of perpetual relationship with God. It now mixes what God has said with what we are saying, and it will later blend our prayers with the prayers of Jesus Christ, heaven's great intercessor. There is no other form of prayer that is more formidable.